Caregiving and COVID-19:
A Critique of Pandemic Privilege

Caregiving and COVID-19:
A Critique of Pandemic Privilege

Austin Mardon
Alexandra Gross
Gina Schopfer
and Elisia Snyder.

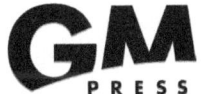

A Golden Meteorite Press Book.
Printed in Canada.

©Copyright 2020, Austin Mardon
Golden Meteorite Press, Edmonton
All rights reserved for *Caregiving and COVID-19: A Critique of Pandemic Privilege* ©.
No part of this publication may be reproduced, stored in any retrieval system, or transmitted in any form or by any means, electronic, mechanical, photocopying, recording, microfilm reproduction and copying, or otherwise, without the prior express written permission of Golden Meteorite Press

First Printing: 2020.

Cover Design and Typesetting by Nicole Schimpf

Telephone: 587-783-0059
Email: aamardon@yahoo.ca
Website: goldenmeteoritepress.com

Additional copies can be ordered from:
Suite 103 11919-82 Street NW
Edmonton, AB
T5B 2W4
CANADA

ISBN: 978-1-77369-150-3 (paperback)

v

Table of Contents

Section One: Introduction 1
    Chapter 1: Gender, Intersectionality and COVID-19 2

Section Two: Caring for Young Children 11
    Chapter 2: Introduction 12
    Chapter 3: Before the Pandemic 17
    Chapter 4: During the Pandemic 24
    Chapter 5: After the Pandemic 31
    Chapter 6: Final Thoughts 37

Section Three: Caring for Seniors 41
    Chapter 7: Introduction 42
    Chapter 8: Before the Pandemic 47
    Chapter 9: During the Pandemic 53
    Chapter 10: After the Pandemic 59
    Chapter 11: Final Thoughts 64

Section Four: Caring for the Chronically Ill and Disabled 69
    Chapter 12: Introduction 70
    Chapter 13: Before the Pandemic 76
    Chapter 14: During the Pandemic 82
    Chapter 15: After the Pandemic 88
    Chapter 16: Final Thoughts 94

Section Five: Caring for Caregivers 101
    Chapter 17: Self-Care Resources for Caregivers 102

Glossary of Terms 110

References 115

Section One:
Introduction

Chapter 1:

Gender, Intersectionality and COVID-19

In 2018, the WHO (World Health Organization) released a handbook titled *Managing Epidemics: Key Facts About Major Deadly Diseases*. The primary purpose of this handbook was to provide instruction to WHO country representatives on responding quickly and efficiently to infectious disease outbreaks (WHO, 2018). At the very beginning of the handbook, the following assertion is made regarding possible future epidemics:

> *Given the effects of globalization, the intense mobility of human populations, and the relentless urbanization, it is likely that the next emerging virus will also spread fast and far. It is impossible to predict the nature of this virus or its source, or where it will start spreading. But we can say, with a high degree of certainty, that when it comes, there will be (a) an initial delay in recognising it; (b) a serious impact on travel and trade; (c) a public reaction that includes anxiety, or even panic and confusion, and (d) this will be aided and abetted by media coverage.* (WHO, 2018, p. 18).

Less than two years later, a new **coronavirus** disease called **COVID-19** emerged and spread both farther and faster than even the WHO could have predicted. The organization failed to initially recognize it for what it was and they delayed declaring it a pandemic for, arguably, much longer than they should have.

While their 2018 prediction did come to fruition, another did not. They stressed that quarantine could no longer be a strategy for fighting epidemics in the 21st century, stating that such a measure would be "unacceptable to many populations today" (WHO, 2018, p. 26). Six months into the pandemic, neither effective treatments nor a vaccine were yet available; quarantine and social distancing measures proved to be the most effective tool in preventing the spread of the virus. These measures required a dramatic societal shift, one that changed the realities of many, not just temporarily, but to some extent permanently. At the time of writing, the pandemic is ongoing. Although we do not yet know what the long term effects will be, it is certain that Canadian society and global relations will not return to the state they were in prior to the pandemic; a new normal will be established. The effects of this new normal will affect different segments of the population in unique ways, and some to a greater extent than others.

One such demographic is composed of caregivers of dependents, and it is their experiences before, during and after the COVID-19 pandemic that will be the focus of this book. The analysis is divided into three primary sections: the experience of carers working from home with children, with elderly adults and with chronically ill and disabled dependents. Each section outlines the major challenges caregivers faced before and during the pandemic and subsequently makes informed post-pandemic predictions. As domestic gender roles and an intersectional framework have implications within each section, an overview of these theories is first required, as well as a background on the COVID-19 pandemic itself.

The COVID-19 Pandemic

Coronavirus Disease 2019, more commonly known as COVID-19, has been touted as "the defining global health crisis of our time and the greatest challenge we have faced since World War Two" (United Nations Development Programme [UNDP], n.d.). COVID-19 is a member of the coronavirus family, within which certain strains affect humans and other animals (Government of Canada [GC], 2020-c). Normally, these diseases do not spread from animals to humans or vice versa and infected persons exhibit mild cold-like symptoms (GC, 2020-c). In the rare case that they do spread from animal to person, they are especially unlikely to subsequently spread from person to person (GC, 2020-c). Two other strains of coronavirus have spread in this manner before, causing significant illness in humans: severe acute respiratory syndrome coronavirus (SARS CoV) and Middle East respiratory syndrome coronavirus (MERS CoV) (GC, 2020-c). Both of these outbreaks were categorized as epidemics, yet even so, they did not spread as quickly and as aggressively as COVID-19.

On December 31st, 2019, authorities from China contacted the WHO about several cases of an unknown illness producing symptoms similar to pneumonia in patients in the city of Wuhan (Kantis et al., 2020). During the month of January of 2020, cases appeared in 23 different countries across Asia, Europe, North America and Australia (Kantis et al., 2020). On January 30th, the WHO publicly declared the outbreak a PHEIC (Public Health Emergency of International Concern). In the month of February, 37 more countries reported their first cases (Kantis et al., 2020). By February 9th, the number of coronavirus deaths had surpassed the total number of deaths during the SARS epidemic, the later of which had lasted about six months (Kantis et al., 2020). It wasn't until March 11th that the WHO finally declared the COVID-19 outbreak a pandemic.

In the following weeks, many nations began to take action. The border between Canada and the United States was closed to all but essential travel. One-third of the entire world's population went into lockdown in the month of March alone (Kantis et al., 2020). It quickly became apparent that there was a significant shortage of medical supplies, and The World Bank released an estimate stating that 11 million individuals would be pushed into poverty as a direct result of the pandemic (Kantis et al., 2020). By the beginning of June, less than six months after the virus was first reported in China, the total number of confirmed cases globally approached seven million (100,000 in Canada), with 188 countries having reported cases and the total number of COVID-19 related deaths nearly hitting the 400,000 mark (approximately 7,800 in Canada) (Kantis et al., 2020).

Much of the fear surrounding the COVID-19 pandemic had arisen from its many unknowns that, at the time of writing, remain to be discovered. Some individuals show severe symptoms to the infection while others do not show any at all, making its spread difficult to track (GC, 2020-c). It is not known how long the virus survives on surfaces or how the virus can be treated. The leading treatment at present is the use of ventilators to help individuals with severe symptoms breathe (GC, 2020-c). Data also seem to suggest that the segment of the population most at risk of experiencing deadly symptoms are the elderly and the health-compromised (GC, 2020-c). Healthy children seem to have the best outcomes, with most not showing any symptoms at all (GC, 2020-c). Immunity and the ability of the disease to mutate is also currently unknown, thus the long term effects of the virus can only be theorized about. As the WHO

(2018) rightly predicted, "anxiety, or even panic and confusion" about the pandemic are keenly felt by the public to this day (p. 18).

Gender and Work

In today's society, we tend to think of women and men as being fairly equal in terms of democratic rights and freedoms. The truth of the matter is that traditional, industrial-age gender roles are still reinforced within both the home and the workplace today. To understand the relationship between gender and work in contemporary Canadian society, a brief overview of this subject's history is first required. The following three paragraphs have been summarized from a discussion on the status of women throughout Canada's history, found within Kimmel & Holler's (2017) book, *The Gendered Society*.

Prior to the nineteenth century, both men and women worked inside of the home. Women, men and children all had very separate, distinct roles within the home. Women took care of the cooking, cleaning and childrearing, while men focused mostly on yard work, repairs, and tending to livestock. Although men held the authority over the family and work roles were distinctly different, women's and men's work was seen as being equally important and respected.

The emergence of the industrial age brought about a dramatic shift: the **separation of the spheres** occurred. Women carried on with their work at home within the private sphere (composed of domestic work and childcare), but men began to engage in paid labour outside of the home within the public sphere (composed of business and politics). Men still held authority over the family, and it was at this point that the status of women began to decline dramatically. Because women's work was unpaid, it was seen as being low in value within the new capitalist society.

During World Wars I and II, women began to leave the private sphere and engage in paid labour outside of the home. This was accepted at the time, as their participation in the labour force filled a need that had been created when working, able-bodied men left their jobs to become soldiers. Along with the right to vote, participation in the labour force was a success of the **first wave of feminism**, wherein women also demanded protection from abuse and the right to attend school, something only boys had been permitted to do until this point. In the post-war period however, women were expected to vacate the roles they had "stolen" from men in the labour force and return to the home. It was at this point that the nuclear, suburban family was born and the stereotypes of breadwinner and homemaker were reinforced. Ultimately, the **second wave of feminism** was born out of this post-war period and the status of women has continued to improve ever since.

Although there has been much improvement since second wave feminism emerged, equality is still far from being achieved. According to Statistics Canada, 82 percent of women in their prime working years are engaged in paid labour within the public sphere (Moyser, 2017). The percentage of married and single women working is roughly equal; a significant improvement in comparison to 1976 when twice as many single women compared to married women worked (Moyser, 2017). Women's participation in postsecondary education is also very high, with 6.5 percent more women obtaining a university degree than men (Moyser, 2017).

However, this is where the improvements end. Although the gap between the percentage of working men and women decreases as educational attainment increases, women's job prospects depend heavily on educational attainment, while men are much more likely to earn a good wage without receiving additional education after high school (Moyser, 2017). Men are more likely to be self-employed than women, and for every dollar they earn, women earn 87 cents - even when controlling for factors such as hours worked per week and the nature of occupation (Moyser, 2017). The types of occupations worked by men and women are also very gendered. Women and men are most likely to work in jobs that are consistent with their traditional gender roles; for women, this means that they are much more likely to work in the service sector (Moyser, 2017). The ten lowest paid occupations are dominated by women, and the ten highest paid occupations are dominated by men, yet men are paid more than women in both categories (Kimmel & Holler, 2017).

This discrepancy makes itself apparent within the private sphere (the home) as well. Because women are still primarily responsible for caring for children, they are much more likely to be employed in part-time work, while men are more likely to be employed in full-time work (Moyser, 2017). Single mothers are less likely to be employed when compared to single fathers and married mothers (Moyser, 2017). The older the youngest child in the family, the more likely the mother is to participate in the labour force; but the age of the youngest child isn't significant to the father's likelihood of participating in the labour force (Moyser, 2017). Although men are spending more time on housework, they are still doing much less than women (Kimmel & Holler, 2017). It is still women who do the majority of the housework, even when they are working full time outside of the home; thus, women come home from work and start a **second shift** of unpaid work (Hochschild & Machung, 1989).

These statistics collectively indicate one major point: women's work is still undervalued today. As women are more likely to be unpaid, informal caregivers within the home, when we discuss the experience of carers working from home with dependents before, during and after the COVID-19 pandemic, we are largely talking about the experience of women.

A Note on Intersectionality

When studying societal issues from a social science perspective, researchers tend to focus on factors that make an individual or group disadvantaged in some way. As we've just discussed, when compared to men, women are more disadvantaged in terms of both paid and unpaid work; this is due to their gender. Social dimensions (such as gender) can be split into categories of privilege and categories of oppression. In this case, the male gender identity receives the most privilege. All other gender identities are subconsciously compared to this "ideal" identity and, falling short of this ideal, they become disadvantaged in one way or another.

This theoretical framework is called **intersectionality**, a term coined by the lawyer and social theorist Kimberle Crenshaw in 1989. The concept of intersectionality originally arose in response to Black women experiencing that the second wave of feminism had no place for them, as it largely reflected the experience of white, middle-class women, which was very different from that of Black women (YW Boston, 2017). While both groups were women, and therefore faced oppression due to their identity as women, the colour of white women's skin afforded them privileges while the colour of Black women's skin oppressed them. Thus, intersectionality reveals the importance of taking into account all dimensions that oppress an individual or group, as they do not exist independently of each other, but rather their relationship is **dialectical** and produces a unique experience (YW Boston, 2017).

The arguments made in the following sections of this book heavily emphasize the concept of intersectionality. The experience of carers is varied, depending on their own intersectional identity, as well as the intersectional identity of their dependents.

10

Section Two:
Caring for Young Children

Chapter 2:

Introduction

The domestic sphere and caregiving to young children has a fraught history in terms of gender. While we are seeing the broader population engage in social isolation due to the COVID-19 pandemic, the home has long been a place of isolation in the more usual sense for women, and especially mothers. When looking at the broad history of women's liberation and suffrage, the main obstacle to gender equality often seems to be the hurdles of both childbearing and childrearing. For white women, this has sometimes meant staying in the house to nurture the children emotionally. For women of colour, this has historically meant **wet-nursing**: nursing another woman's baby either for reasons either medical or social in nature.

White women historically looked down on nursing their own children because it was seen to be demeaning or a task for a lower class of citizen; however, they seemed to have no qualms spending time with their children. In this way, women of colour were kept in the home for reasons both social and economic. Wet-nursing and childrearing were seen to be women's work, and women's work was best done at home. As we begin to think about the role of a caregiver and caring for young children, it behoves the authors to think about the ongoing history of unpaid domestic labour by women, particularly because this is a narrative that is thought to be *only* historical rather than current. The *London Review* notes in an article from 4 June, 2020 that "with schools closed, 45 [percent] of men say they are spending more time home-schooling than their wives. Three [percent] of women say their husbands are spending more time home-schooling than they themselves are" (London Review, 2020).
Women are entering the workforce at a far greater rate now than ever before. Dual income households have been all but necessary to survive and

are far more secure in a time when the Canadian unemployment rate has increased to nearly 14 percent (Statistics Canada, 2020). The average price of groceries has spiked somewhere between 2 and 4 percent since the beginning of the pandemic, leaving families short on disposable income for commodities like toys, games and art supplies, clothes, footwear, and outerwear for their children (Canada's Food Price Report, 2020). In Canada, where the weather can change at the metaphorical drop of a hat, the need for appropriate clothing to suit the weather is paramount, especially if one finds themselves and their family out of doors.

Students of psychology will be familiar with **Maslow's Hierarchy of Needs:** an infographic developed by Charles Maslow that outlines not only the needs that each individual has, but also the degree of urgency each of those needs has in comparison to the other needs. While this framework of understanding human psychology is rather simplistic and mildly contested, it offers a solid starting point from which we can begin to discuss an individual's needs.

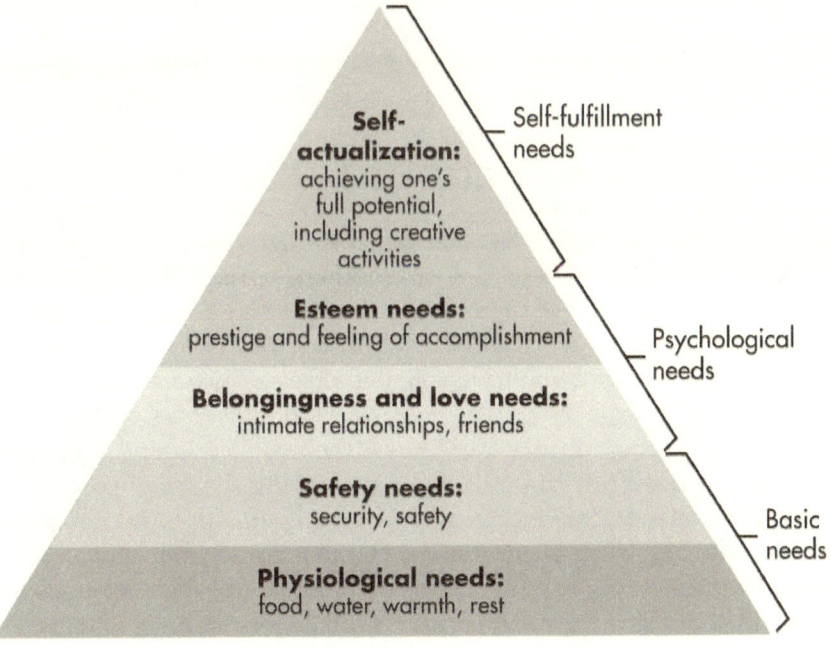

Broadly speaking, human beings need food, shelter, comfort, and purpose. Beginning with food, any caregiver to a child knows how difficult it is to get little ones to eat their vegetables. A few things make it especially difficult for many children to eat a healthy and balanced diet, their proclivity for sugar being only one of many barriers. Canadian children depend on international supply chains to ensure that they have access to fresh produce of all kinds. In fact, 17 percent of the agricultural imports from the United States into Canada consist of fresh produce (Minnesota Dept. of Agriculture, 2016). Whether it is avocados from Mexico or oranges from California, even the most accessible Canadian cities are dependent on world trade for their nutritional wellbeing.

Canadian children in more northern climates, such as the Northwest Territories and the Yukon territories, have a far greater difficulty obtaining fresh goods, and do so only at great financial expense. This is a problem exacerbated by the demographics of these hard-to-reach places on the map. According to Statistics Canada, "the Northwest Territories had the youngest population after Nunavut. Approximately one person in five (21.4%) living in this territory was under 15 years of age, while only six persons in 100 (6.2%) were aged 65 and over" (Statistics Canada, 2020). According to the same report, Nunavut has an even younger population with approximately a third of the population being under 15 years of age (Statistics Canada, 2020).

Children's nutrition from an early age plays an important role not only in their development, but also in the strength of their immune systems. Having a strong immune system is important in the North where a person's body needs to be at full strength to survive the elements, cope with deficiencies in Vitamin D from minimal sunlight, and resist contagious diseases when in close-quarters with others during the long winters. Missing out on those leafy green vegetables puts children at risk for viral infections, including the flu, and likely also COVID-19. Throw a picky eater into the mix and you have yourself a recipe for potential illness.

The next need that Maslow identifies is the need for safety. After just a few months of self-isolation in the home during the novel coronavirus pandemic, cases of domestic violence had spiked. Not only were people being locked up with their abusers in their homes, but the measures taken by many support networks to maintain social distancing also resulted in the reduced availability of resources for the men, women, and children suffering from domestic violence. This can be a living hell for some people, 24 hours per day. It should be noted here that as of May 2020, there was a 34 percent increase in the number of men accessing domestic violence resources at a shelter in Calgary, Alberta (Calgary's Emergency Women's Shelter, 2020). Whereas before the pandemic, people could reach out to help-lines while their abuser was away for work or out on a social call, the new reality of being locked inside all day meant near constant surveillance. This type of environment can be damaging for children to witness, even in cases where the abuse is not directed at them as such.

Domestic violence was not the only threat to children's physical safety in the domestic sphere during this time of global crisis. Many shelters, community pantries, and other public service centers closed their doors due to health concerns. Those services, which often saw crowding in their waiting areas, are tricky to provide while still maintaining safe physical distancing measures. While it is important to make sure that all individuals who need these services have access to them, children are especially of importance because their minds, bodies, and attitudes about the world around them are still developing.

Children have the additional need of socialization for learning purposes, whereas adults tend to engage in socialization mainly for companionship. The old cliché is as true as ever: children are like sponges. They pick up on their caregivers' vocabulary and mannerisms, but they need to learn these elements of social interaction from their peer group as well. While adults may learn new vocabulary from their peers (and from their children) occasionally, children as young as two are believed to be constantly engaged in a process termed **fast-mapping**.

Fast-mapping is the process by which children as young as two years of age develop knowledge of a concept through minimal exposure (Wikipedia). This concept is particularly important to language development, as children who are fast-mapping may learn as many as 140 new words per week. Developers of AI sometimes turn to children's natural propensity for fast-mapping when they are trying to train machines to learn languages. Studies show that, when children are not properly socialized, their ability to learn language (or their ability to take instruction and learn other information) is severely hindered, especially if the variety of language that the child is exposed to is limited. A study from Princeton in 2016 found that "children at the lower end of the [socioeconomic] spectrum tend to receive significantly less high-quantity and high-quality language experience, which affects their development of vocabulary, grammar, and language processing" (Schwab and Lew-Williams, 2016.)

Children who have been poorly socialized are likely to exhibit poor academic performance and development, which may in turn lead to low self-esteem. Children who do not have the opportunity to socialize cannot learn from one another, nor do they have the opportunity to learn about themselves by comparison. It may be a nasty habit for adults to "keep up with the Jones," but the reality for children is that they need peer engagement to begin engaging in self-reflection and, in turn, develop healthy levels of self-esteem.

One of the healthy ways that children do this is through competition. Having a race to the swing set or seeing who can throw a baseball the furthest lets children develop a rudimentary metric of how they can begin to estimate their abilities. This is not to say that a child needs to perform well at everything to have high self-esteem, but rather that children need to be exposed to a wide range of activities to find their likes and dislikes, as well as their natural talents, including artistic endeavors.

While children are at home with their parents in quarantine, they cannot create a fair estimation of how well they perform at activities as compared to their peers. The only point of comparison available are the caregivers themselves. For example, a child comparing their hand-eye coordination through the process of drawing to that of an adult may teach them that they are not a competent drawer, (even if they are adequate for their age). This unfair comparison could lead to low self-esteem, which could lead to self-destructive behaviours.

The goal is ultimately **self-actualization**: helping children learn who they are, be proud of who they are, and develop the character and work ethic necessary for them to conceptualize and realize their goals and dreams. The world we now face may make some of those dreams difficult. However, examining how this world has changed for children may help their caregivers approach the challenges of providing the best care possible to give the leaders of tomorrow the tools for self-actualization and the possibility of a safe and healthy future.

Chapter 3:

Before the Pandemic

Before the COVID-19 pandemic, caring for children in 21st century Canada was an ongoing community effort. While Canada is a wealthy nation, even single-child families often feel the pressure to have two incomes to pay bills and afford a comfortable and safe home life. The desire to go on family vacations to tropical destinations has also been a strong incentive to have a two-income household in Canada, where the winters are harsh and long. Even in ideal financial circumstances where two parents are working, raising one or more children while balancing two work schedules can be logistically challenging.

In many cases, Canadians have used external childcare, such as day homes or day cares; families with more expendable income have opted to hire live-in childcare. Alternatively, many families have relied on their own relatives. The children's grandparents have typically been the top option for a number of reasons. First, in cases where two sets of grandparents live close by with whom the parents have a positive relationship, there is a built-in flexibility to the childcare schedule. Out of four people who may be retired, working shifts, working part-time, or working from a home office, the likelihood that someone is available at any given moment is good. The odds can be even better when reliable aunts or uncles are in that rotation. Childcare even before the pandemic was less of an issue for school-aged children than it has been for younger children, so long as the children could be dropped off and picked up at the beginning and of the day, respectively. This task could usually be taken on by one or alternating parents.

Research suggests that the "majority of working women have a dual-role as both wage-earner and domestic worker," (Pickup, 1984) and that tasks such as household shopping, balancing the family budget, and domestic labour such as cleaning and childrearing have been primarily left to women in heterosexual, two-parent households where both parents work. Historically, this has been more difficult for women, who have a gendered history of low travel mobility. Having a license, let alone having a car available to them during the day, has been rare for women. City-dwelling caregivers with access to public transportation have made ample use of its service. However, even with the advent of women entering the workforce at higher rates, and the increase of urban sprawl--leaving many households with long commutes from their residence to their workplace--the task of arranging transportation for children has still been primarily left to female caregivers, whether it be through bussing, walking, or driving. The same rotation of relatives who may have cared for the children before they were school-aged may also have taken on these pick-up/drop-off tasks. Older children have often taken part in bearing this responsibility as well, especially in single-parent homes. In one study, researchers observed that:

> *...adult/child dichotomies have dominated sociology and the assumption is often made that children are an undifferentiated category, with the effect that disparities within the broad category, whether along the lines of gender, ethnicity, class and age, are obscured... this social construction of children and childhood effectively renders children's labour outside school 'invisible.'* (Mayall, 1994).

Males have been more likely (Moyser and Burlock, 2018) to contract or outsource domestic labour (including housework, childcare, and meal preparation) to caregivers, whereas women—who have historically earned less on the dollar per hour than men—are statistically more likely to take on domestic work themselves in order to save money as well as to cement familial relationships. Of course, there has always been more to raising children than ping-ponging them around to caregivers and cleaning up after them. Children have diverse social, personal, hygienic, psychological, cognitive, and nutritional needs even when they are neuro-typical and meeting or exceeding average developmental milestones.

Hygiene

Even before the world had heard of the novel coronavirus, hand hygiene was a major concern for young children. Elementary schools are a breeding ground for the flu as well as other contagious health concerns, such as head lice. An article from 2008 in the *Journal of School Health* titled "Inexpensive and Time-Efficient Hand Hygiene Interventions Increase Elementary School Children's Hand Hygiene Rates" by Snow et al suggests that a simple demonstration of hand-washing and a reminder from a caregiver can increase rates of hand hygiene among children. Young children (grade one) were more likely to listen to instruction and develop good hand-washing habits, whereas older children (grades five to six) were less likely to maintain hand hygiene unless they were being monitored and reminded more than once to wash their hands. Hand washing and alcohol-based sanitizers remain an effective method for keeping hands clean after touching common surfaces, such as door knobs, tablets, tables, chairs, and keyboards.

Another way to keep children healthy has been to stay current on vaccinations. Vaccinations have been important not only to a child's individual health, but also to the health of their peer groups because of "**community immunity**;" germs can travel quickly through a community, making many members of that community sick. If enough people contract the sickness, it can lead to an epidemic. Fortunately, when most members of a community are vaccinated against a certain disease, germs cannot travel as easily from person to person — and the entire community is less likely to spread the disease.

In recent years, a movement known as the **anti-vax movement** has spread fear amongst caregivers of young children that vaccinations are not only not beneficial, but also potentially dangerous. Some anti-vaxxers believe that having a child vaccinated against viral infections can cause autism spectrum disorder. There is no known scientific evidence to substantiate this claim. All said, even proper hand hygiene and vaccinations do not offer enough protection if a child's immune system is too weak. For children who are not immunocompromised, a strong immune system begins with proper nutrition.

Nutrition

As mentioned in the introduction to this section, Canadians rely on global supply chains to maintain a healthy diet supplemented with enough fresh produce to maintain their immune systems. For Canadians, a lack of Vitamin D due to limited exposure to sunlight can have significant impacts on immune system health. From the time that children are between six and nine months old, they show signs of being ready to take solid foods. These signs (*Pediatric Nutritional Guidelines*, 2016) may include the following:

1. Developing better head control
2. Sitting up and leaning forward
3. Signaling to the caregiver when they are full (e.g. turns head away)
4. Can pick up food and try to put it in their mouth
5. Has vertical jaw movement (munching)
6. Has some tongue protrusion when beginning to eat solid foods which decreases with experience
7. May still have early gag reflex until around seven months
8. Often rejects unfamiliar foods a number of times

As children get older and begin to be able to feed themselves, their food intake becomes less predictable, more erratic, and highly influenced by the foods that the caregivers themselves eat. The main food advisory concerning children pre-pandemic is that they eat the right foods; foods should be nutrient-dense, fully cooked, and low in sugar. Eggs, shellfish, deli-meats, sprouts, and unpasteurized dairy products are not recommended for young children due to concerns that bacterial infections could present.

The main thing to remember here is that "Parents and other caregivers shape the development of children's eating behaviours, not only by the foods they make available to children, but also by their own eating styles, behaviour at mealtimes, and child feeding practices. Parents'/ caregivers' child-feeding practices are critical for children developing healthy eating habits later in life" (Pediatric Nutritional Guidelines, 2016, p. 12). Feeding should be responsive to childrens' level of appetite, accommodating any allergies, and critical of shyness to try new foods; however, coerciveness regarding the amount of food intake may lead to unhealthy eating or attitudes about food. When children are encouraged to self-regulate their diet as it pertains to their hunger, but also guided into eating nutritious foods, a healthy diet is likely to be the result.

Cognitive Wellbeing

Cognitive development in children is an important area of study, and an area well-traipsed by the psychological pioneer, Jean Piaget. Piaget drew a distinction between "development" and "learning" in his 1964 paper on the subject of cognitive development in children. In his view, "development" was the endpoint of **embryogenesis**, the time at which the nervous system is finished developing physiologically. Learning, by contrast, was an event provoked by a situation or a teacher, and limited to a problem and a solution. According to Piaget, development explained learning but was not the same as learning.

Piaget's view of cognitive wellbeing is perhaps what we now understand as deriving from an ableist perspective. His belief that learning is fundamentally tied to neuro-typical development is, to say the least, a problematic one. Despite this, his concepts create a valuable starting point for a conversation around learning and development in children and allow us to differentiate these concepts from the later discussion around mental health.

Cognitive wellbeing and learning have mainly been under the domain of schools and teachers. A parent may teach their preschool-aged children the alphabet, numbers, basic shapes, colours, and patterns, but teachers within the school system do most of the heavy lifting in terms of caring for the cognitive wellbeing and development of society's young children. The conventional wisdom for parents has been to get children away from screens with over-stimulating visual and auditory sensations and to try to get children to instead engage in kinetic, athletic, or sensory play. Either making concoctions with household items, running around outside with other children, or tinkering with blocks, learning toys stimulate a child's mind and encourage them to be curious and intellectual young thinkers.

Some children need more stimulation than others. Boredom is perhaps the enemy of all parents with young children. If there is more than one child in the house, the built-in social aspect of having a sibling can abate some of the ire of boredom. Boredom can also be a productive parenting tool, as it gives children the opportunity to think about how they would like to fill their time. Before the pandemic, many public recreational facilities such as movie theaters, aquariums, museums, amusement parks, and public beaches were available for caregivers and children to share their time together. Social outings created their own form of stimuli that are essential to learning.

Part of the process of taking in stimuli in the outside world was to prevent **overdetermination** in language. Overdetermination refers to when a speaker uses a word with a single meaning to describe a separate object or idea. For example, a child with knowledge of dogs might use the word "dog" to describe all four-legged animals. Exposure to new stimuli allows caregivers to correct those metaphysical, epistemological, and linguistic errors early on. The same is true for learning about other cultures and people. Healthy attitudes about differences in age, sex, race, gender-identity, and ability are all learned through proper exposure to diverse types of people.

Mental Health

Mental health should not be confused with cognitive wellbeing. Although both are matters of the mind, cognitive wellbeing is chiefly concerned with the agility of the mind to accept and categorize new stimuli and to solve theoretical problems. Mental health, by contrast, is a matter of personal comfort, and the brain's ability to cope with the unfamiliar or with personally applicable practical problem situations. Despite the name, mental health is closely tied to physiological health, including nutrition and sleep hygiene.

Before the pandemic, meals and sleep were structured around the tasks of the day: waking up for school or for childcare and getting to sleep on time to do it all again the next day were arranged around the working schedules of parental figures. Socializing and meeting the challenges of learning in school or out in the community were all part of building a child's confidence. Children being raised in a city or suburbs learned to grow in confidence navigating city life (transit, crowded places, shopping centres, playdates with other children, and knowing how to stay safe around strangers), and children growing up in rural areas would grow in confidence by finding their ways around farm equipment, cattle, camping gear, and farm pets.

In Canada, some children live on Indigenous reservations. There has been an ongoing public health crisis on reservations, particularly in the northern regions of the country, where the mental health of Indigenous youth has suffered as a result of intergenerational trauma. Whether this trauma has been passed as a result of grandparents who survived the genocidal effects of the residential school system, the damage to people who are now parents as a result of the 60s scoop, the ongoing effects of the foster care system's interference with Indigenous families, or a combination of all of the above, the tragic effect has been an epidemic of suicides amidst Indigenous youth who live on reservation.

An article on the CBC website dated November 23, 2019 indicates that "seven people from the [Makwa Sahgaiehcan First Nation] have taken their own lives since 2016...including a 10-year old girl." The lack of medical care on and near reservations, the number of Indigenous women and girls who go missing and are found murdered each year, and systemic, government-sanctioned discrimination against Indigenous people in this country surely all contribute in part to the ailing mental health of Indigenous youth on Turtle Island and numerous other Indigenous communities across Canada.

Chapter 4:

During the Pandemic

Having now discussed the state of caregiving for children before the novel coronavirus pandemic struck, we can begin to discuss the ways in which the pandemic has changed life for many Canadians caregivers of young children. The main challenge that families face is adjusting to the intrusion of home life into other aspects of their lives. Many adults who used to go into work every day are "spending more time with their children": a popular new phrase that plays fast and loose with the definition of "spending time".

Many families do not have the luxury of using the time spent in quarantine on quality shared time with their young children. Parents and caregivers who are working remotely are faced with creating a home office environment and somehow explaining to their children that while, "yes I am home more, I cannot play with you more". Two-parent families may be able to take shifts watching their children, splitting up their day into manageable chunks (but perhaps extending their workdays to make up for lost time). If the children are school-aged, parents and caregivers may find themselves taking on the added role of tutor while the children are taking their lessons online. Many families are struggling to manage internet sharing, with both parents and children all using up the bandwidth. Connections can be slow and work can take longer to get done than it would if only one person were working or schooling from home.

Some families are faced with additional challenges. The number of Canadians who signed up for financial government assistance through the Canada Emergency Response Benefit (CERB) as of the week of June 15th, 2020 was approximately 524,420 people (Statistics Canada). These data represent people who are or have been receiving $2,000 per month, per person since this benefit plan was announced on March 25th, 2020. The families who received CERB funding may be expected to pay it back once they are again able to secure full-time employment.

Until then, they have to live on this reduced income that may not pay all of the bills. Families with children may be facing the pressures of looking for work while also performing the tasks of childcare, as well as stand-in school teaching. Families who cannot pay their bills and are forced into bankruptcy may need to sell their home - another task that proves especially difficult during uncertain economic times.

Fortunately, it is not all doom and gloom. Many families are finding that they are saving money by working from home, doing their own childcare (thereby saving on childcare costs), avoid commuting to and from work (saving on gas, plus wear and tear on vehicles), and avoiding expensive leisure activities such as going out to eat or going to a public recreational facility. It has certainly been possible for some to save money by cutting back on non-essential activities.

The changes in the daily lives of children and their caregivers has been one of the most notable effects of the COVID-19 crisis. In this chapter, we will examine the same areas of interest that we discussed in the last chapter; however, we will be not only focusing on the state of matters, but also on how caregivers can approach what many are calling the "new normal". Again, we will be looking at nutrition, hygiene, cognitive wellness, and mental health. This chapter will make suggestions as to how caregivers can explain the situation to young children, and help both parties adjust to social and physical distancing guidelines and life in social isolation, as well as think about community safety.

Hygiene

As discussed in the introduction, COVID-19 is a viral respiratory illness that spreads mainly through droplets of effluvia ejected from the nose and mouth. The virus consists of ribonucleic acid encased in a lipid/protein envelope. The most effective known methods for the general population for avoiding infection and community spread include frequent handwashing with soap and warm water, wearing a disposable or washable fabric nonmedical mask, using hand sanitizer products that contain over 60 percent alcohol content, and standing at least 6 feet (2 metres) apart in order.

The lipid encasing of the virus can be destroyed by soap and water, rendering the virus unable to survive long enough to transfer on surfaces. Wearing a mask restricts the transmission of droplets, but only in a limited manner. If only one party is wearing a mask in any given situation, the chances of transmission increase. When all parties are wearing masks, the transmission rate is reduced significantly.

COVID-19 is currently thought to be able to survive on surfaces for a span between eight and seventy-two hours, but no definitive evidence that this is true exists. Sanitization products such as Spray Nine can effectively reduce the amount of viral material on surfaces. Wiping down surfaces combined with frequent handwashing have been found to be effective in reducing the spread of infection.

To date, there are no available vaccinations against the novel coronavirus. Caregivers are recommended to wash their hands and the food and packaging of items from the grocery store. Old habits are hard to break and people still frequently touch produce with their bare hands. A quick wash with soapy water can help guard against infection. People are also encouraged to cough or sneeze into the crook of their elbows to avoid handshakes, and to keep physical contact to a minimum where possible.

For children, the transition to frequent handwashing can be challenging. As discussed last chapter, young children are more likely to listen to instruction and develop good habits early on. That said, young children also tend to have sensitive skin. Frequent hand washing can lead to cracks or breaks in the skin. If parents are finding that frequent hand washing is leading to skin breakdown, applying a non-perfumed lotion is advisable. Health professionals have been ubiquitously reminding the public that hand sanitizing products are not a suitable substitute for washing hands with soap and water, though they should be used immediately after contact with public surfaces, such as those found at a grocery store.

An effective method of getting young children to wash their hands thoroughly is to sing a song with them as they wash their hands. The length of the alphabet song is about the recommended amount of time that children should be washing their hands. Singing the alphabet (as opposed to Happy Birthday or Twinkle Twinkle Little Star) has the added bonus of helping children learn their letters. If the child in your care already knows the alphabet, a recommended substitute is singing the names of the planets, the tune for which can be found on YouTube.

Nutrition

As is the case with many areas of study surrounding COVID-19, it is too soon to have accurate data on how the virus has affected pediatric nutrition. As far as infants are concerned, it is believed that the virus does not transmit through breast milk. New mothers can protect newborn babies by using the hygiene guidelines outlined in this chapter. Hand hygiene is especially important during feeding, whether that is through breastfeeding or with bottled formula. New parents who are unable to access donor breast milk in the event that home-pumped breast milk is unavailable are advised to use bottled formula or to consult their family doctor.

It is not uncommon for new mothers to have difficulty breastfeeding or producing milk within the first several days after labour. This is especially true of women who have undergone a cesarean section operation. This is no cause for panic. Mothers who cannot produce breast milk in the first few days after labour may fear that their new baby will starve or suffer severe side effects from malnutrition; however, manual stimulation of the breasts is likely to produce milk within a few days. If not, bottled formula serves as an effective substitute until milk production begins.

Buying baby formula and other groceries should be restricted to one member of the household when possible. The social situation of going to the grocery store is riddled with opportunities for community transmission of the virus, from touching products to the exposure of droplets. Canadians face the precarious situation of international supply chains remaining open while borders for travel remain largely closed across the globe. That being said, Canada has some of the most arable soil in the world.

Growing vegetables and fruits at home serves the triple purpose of creating an activity while in isolation while also providing fresh food and saving money on marked-up grocery store items. Teaching children about gardening is an excellent way to communicate nutritional education and sometimes helps picky eaters find an incentive to try new foods. Speaking from personal experience, a certain four-year old who only likes white bread and noodles tried kale and basil from our home garden for the first time because she was involved in the planting. The benefits go on and on.

Even for individuals who live in the city who do not have backyards, the ability to grow herbs and smaller plants in the window presents an opportunity for learning and growth. Community gardens are becoming more and more common in cities and even smaller Canadian towns. Caregivers can take small children to community gardens or You-Pick farms to see where their food comes from. I would encourage every person reading this book to take the time to see if there is a farm-share program that delivers to their neighbourhood. Contactless delivery is increasingly an option for both farm-share programs and grocery stores. Delivery of groceries has been and continues to be a great alternative for people with limited mobility, including people who do not have an available car or a driver's license.

Cognitive Wellbeing

If cognitive wellbeing is looked at as a metric for mental agility, the effects of keeping children out of school in order to distance themselves physically from their classmates must be considered. Caregivers in many families are expected to now be both breadwinners and home tutors. The number of children in the household, the education-level of the caregiver, and the amount of time that the caregiver spends on educational activities will all impact the quality of cognitive engagement that the children are receiving, and the rate at which the child progresses both academically (learning) and developmentally. As has already been stressed, making nutritional and hygienic education a part of childrens' at-home education can be productive for cognitive development. At the time of writing, many teachers are coming up with creative assignments for their students. It is important to avoid undermining the efforts of the educational professionals in the child's life, as this could be more confusing than helpful; however, some caregivers do need to step in from time to time to teach children about non-academic life skills and lessons.

As the pandemic marches on, it has become increasingly necessary for caregivers to educate children about viruses and illnesses. Children are naturally curious and, especially if they're already verbal, will eventually have questions about why things are so different than they used to be. It is important to speak to children according to their level of understanding and to avoid simplifying matters too much (creating potentially unsafe behaviours due to assumed low levels of risk) or too little (creating confusion). A study titled "Development of Children's Concepts of Illness" conducted by Dr. Roger Bibace and Dr. Mary E. Walsh in the Department of Psychology at Clark University in Massachusetts examines Piaget and Werner's stages of cognitive development and uses their findings to create a model that "can be useful to [caregivers] (1) in explaining illness and providing "reassurance" to children, (2) in developing meaningful health education strategies, and (3) in responding to the degree of control the child feels over the illness" (Bibace and Walsh, 1980).

For children between the ages of two and six, children will accept "pre-logical" explanations of illness (Bibace and Walsh). That is, they will accept any explanation as to why there is a global pandemic, but that is not the important aspect. The important aspect is that children need to be informed that *there is* a virus spreading and that they need to practice safe behaviors. Older children between the ages of seven and ten will accept "concrete-logical" explanations (Bibace and Walsh); they understand the concept of contamination and will understand *why* viruses are contagious, though they still fail to understand how viruses work inside the body. Lastly, children of about 11 years and older tend to require "formal-logical" explanations (Bibace and Walsh). They tend to understand why and how viruses spread and they also can interpret how individual physical and psychophysical behaviours affect health - for example, they know that stress and sleep patterns are part of physical and psychological health.

It is important that caregivers stay engaged with children under their care. Young children perceive adult business as purposeful ignoring and may feel hurt or think that their caregiver is angry with them if the caregiver is not making time for them. At the same time, solitary play is beneficial for cognitive development. It stimulates the imagination and allows children to create their own fun and begin to cope with their own boredom. Giving a child instructions, a full set of required items, a task and a goal are all great ways to encourage children to engage in solitary play. A puzzle, a craft, a model plane or train, a concoction of age-appropriate household items, or even dolls can start a child off. Workbooks designed for a specific age group with lessons on math, letters, or phonics are also a good investment.

Mental Health

The mental health of children during this difficult time in human history is a delicate matter that will be unique to every individual. A good way of assessing and responding to the mental health of the child under care is to create age-appropriate metrics that *they* can use to communicate with their caregiver. If the child is behaving in a way that seems unusual when compared to their normal personality, the caregiver should ask them to show how they feel using a numerical scale or a qualitative scale. For example, a carer can ask if they have any *big* problems or any *little* problems or how happy they are on a scale from zero to ten. It is important to encourage children to use their words and express their feelings without fear of punishment.

Many caregivers misstep by asking children who do finally express their feelings the unanswerable question: "why didn't you tell me?". Too often, children do not have the words to express themselves and need adult guidance to draw them out. Using deep-breathing exercises paired with counting can be a good way to help children pair their cognitive and mental wellbeing with a simultaneous coping mechanism. Too much stress can be distracting to learning and harmful for emotional development. It is the responsibility of caregivers to recognize reclusive and aggressive behaviours and to speak calmly to the child to understand what is triggering the changes in behaviour.

Importantly, some children are naturally introverted or boisterous. When looking for red flags to poor mental health, caregivers should be looking for sudden changes that have negative side-effects for the child. If a child, for example, starts spending a little more time in their room than usual, this is not cause for concern. Some changes are natural to maturing, or appropriate responses to environmental stimuli. Communicating with the child is the key to nurturing their mental health alongside them.

Chapter 5:

After the Pandemic

At the time of writing, the long-term effects of the pandemic are still unknown. Like other major world events, the impacts on the worldviews of future generations will be many and multifaceted. The same way that commercial air travel has never been the same for North Americans after the tragic events of September 11th, 2001, the world will also never forget the devastating loss of human life, nor the ruinous effects on the global economy caused by the international outbreak of this viral infection.

For children growing up during this time, the world has not fundamentally "changed" the way that it has changed for adults who were used to commuting to work, sharing food from buffet tables, and rubbing shoulders at large gatherings in public places. For children, it will likely be "normal" to wear masks in public places, to avoid touching items in stores that they do not plan on purchasing, to stand at a physical distance from strangers, and to wash their hands frequently.

One of the most amazing things about children is that the psycholinguistic tools that they have to learn "language" also help them to develop mental concepts and make sense of things that were previously uncategorized. For example, when children are introduced to a bilingual environment, they will come up with what is called a "Pidgin" language - an often chaotic mishmash of words and phrases from the two languages they heard growing up. But a generation later, the children of the "Pidgin" speakers will develop a "Creole" language, which is a true language that is grammatically correct and functional. In a manner of speaking, tomorrow's children will be able to parse the "new language" of the virus. They will see the clunky example of their caregivers who are stuck half in their old normal and half in their new normal; they will learn to smooth out the gaps in the system; and they will eventually become accustomed to a world where respiratory health is not taken for granted.

It is difficult to begin imagining "the end of this pandemic" for a few reasons. The first is that there is still no vaccine available. Secondly, even if there were a vaccine available, predictions about the methods of consumption and distribution are widely disputed; at least one source suggests that the effort to vaccinate against the novel coronavirus "could rival the urgent national campaign to vaccinate children against polio in the 1950s" (Owermohle, 2020). Because the virus is a respiratory illness, it is unclear what form a vaccine would take, be it intravenous drug, an inhaler that functions by atomizing a vaccine directly to the lungs, or some yet unthought of method.

In the case where an intravenous injection is used to distribute the vaccine via hypodermic needle, the environmental impact of using and disposing of one-use plastics on such a mass scale would be disastrous. Additionally, the specialized medical-grade glass mined from riverbeds and used to store vaccines has been in short supply since before the outbreak. Scaling up the production of a vaccine could jeopardize the supply levels of medical-grade materials for other needs in hospitals, including sedatives.

It is difficult to say how the shift in hospital resources will impact the health and safety of future children, and especially children who are being born in potentially understocked maternity wards. Some children who would have had access to donor breast milk may no longer have that same access. We may see a significant increase in children who were fed bottled formula at unprecedented rates. Many studies have shown that breast milk has unique benefits as compared to formula. Whether this means future children will be underdeveloped or that manufacturers of formula will step up their game is impossible to say. We can speculate on a few of the aspects that we discussed in this chapter and imagine what the world might be like for children whose futures will be shaped fundamentally by the limits imposed by the threat of ultra-contagious respiratory failure.

Hygiene

It seems likely that engineering will step in to create more sanitary public environments where children play and learn. Social engineering can already be seen in grocery stores where indicators on the floor show in which directions shoppers should be walking the aisles as well as at what distance they should stand apart. Furthermore, transparent face shields are a new and likely permanent fixture for cashiers and other public-facing employees. It well may be that childcare facilities will adopt some form of social engineering built into play spaces.

Some teachers interviewed for this book suggested that elementary school-aged children - whose learning is mainly kinetic and sensory, and not suited to online transmittal - will enforce smaller class sizes by alternating education days. That is, children will be organized into quarantine-size groups (roughly 15 students, or half of a regular class) whose school days will be limited to specific days of the week. Future children thus may, in effect, never meet most of their "classmates". Smaller class sizes may allow teachers to offer more individualized learning to each child as a result of decreasing class sizes. It also could be that the play areas themselves are engineered to keep children physically distant from one another, even during free playtime. The result of so much social engineering is impossible to predict, but it is sure to have a lifelong effect.

Common wisdom often dictates that it is beneficial for children to be exposed to bacteria and some pathogens in order to build up a natural level of immunity. Perfectly sanitized areas of school and play may actually weaken the immune systems of children, though an alternative to such an environment is not immediately apparent under the circumstances. The advent of a world of touch-screen technology has tremendously backfired in the arena of hand hygiene. Schools are quick to adapt by replacing physical touch with hands to distanced modes of touch via long sticks with soft material adhered to the end to activate touch screen smart boards. This method seems to the writer a bit clumsy and roundabout. It may be more straightforward to return to the older technologies of markers and whiteboards, or blackboards and chalk (though perhaps equally poor for respiratory health).

Nutrition

With the mass number of Canadians on subsidized income through the CERB fund, it is probable that people will reduce their spending on dining out. Not only has the pandemic already forced people to reconsider frivolous spending, but it has also massively impacted the restaurant and hospitality industry to the point where many sit-down restaurants can no longer afford to keep their doors open. Sitting and eating out, as many Canadians have done in the past, is becoming less and less popular due to the chances for community spread through utensils, flatware, and close seating. While restrictions on restaurants place their seating at about half capacity, many restaurants are lucky to seat that many. Furthermore, restaurant staff have been more likely than restaurant patrons to catch the virus, which has been leading to restaurant shutdowns for safety reasons. Although many restaurants are flourishing by using a curb-side pickup model of distribution, it seems that eating dinner at home is the most cost-effective way to be eating in a time when disposable income is scarce. It would be helpful to see the curb-side pickup model evolve for other services, such as donor breast milk.

As for actual pediatric nutritional intake, home-cooked meals are generally less processed and therefore more healthy than take-out from restaurants. As more people turn to their gardens for sustenance, Canadians may return to canning vegetables and perhaps also smoking meats to last through the harsh winters. It will become increasingly important to sanitize goods from the grocery store, creating even further incentive to grow or locally source goods. Though we will likely see more efficient supply chains as we whittle down to the essentials, we may also see certain foods gaining more cultural value than they had before. Foods that are cheap, easy to access, and easy to make will probably become staple foods for caregivers; new family favourites will be born, and the memories associated with these childhood foods will last a lifetime.

While Americans have faced an obesity crisis far worse than Canadians have seen, the fast-food industry has been alive and well in this country. Some estimates suggest that roughly one in three Canadian adults (ObesityinCanada.ca, 2020) struggle with obesity. And where adults trod, children will follow. Children learn their nutritional habits from their caregivers. As the current pandemic marches on and as new or mutated versions of the novel coronavirus may present globally, diets consisting of dark leafy greens and high levels of vitamins and minerals will be needed to safeguard children and the people with whom they interact.

Cognitive Wellbeing

It could be that future models of schooling will bring about more individualized programs with increased parental involvement. For the current classes of 2020, many students in all levels of schooling have simply been processed through with a "pass" for the last half of their academic years while educators regroup and plan for the upcoming Fall 2020 and Winter 2021 terms. Smaller social groups could lead to more meaningful social engagement. By the same token, smaller social groups could lead to conformity for fear of not being a member of the peer group with the few friends who are in social contact.

More focused attention could also lead to increased pressure to perform well academically. Educators and caregivers should be mindful in the future about the kinds of stresses that learning from home and learning in small, focused classes can create. Alternatively, caregivers working from home may try to take advantage of the time that they have with the children in their care, leading to a less structured and rigorous model of education. Home-schooling can lead to more time spent helping around the house and learning about household chores, daily tasks, or even the responsibilities that the adults in the world are accountable for, such as balancing the household budget. A less academic, more practical model of learning may spawn from more time spent at home. A resentment for overly complicated and non-essential learning material may crop up with parents. More academically-oriented and involved parents may decide to accelerate their childrens' education beyond their grade level, if the child is mentally equipped to do so.

Mental Health

The COVID-19 pandemic has given individuals ample opportunity to step back from their work lives and reassess their lifestyle and values. One effect of time spent away from work has been the flexibility for people to become politically involved in matters of global interest, including racial equality and representation. With more "free" time to let the mind explore, families are becoming more educated on matters of social justice, and with that comes the freedom for underrepresented members of society to voice their mental health concerns, including fear for safety due to police brutality.

Black and Indigenous individuals and other racialized groups tend to suffer from mental health issues in this country and across North America. The increase in free time may allow more people to engage in political justice and could also lead to more positive mental health outcomes for those same groups. Fear for physical safety that sometimes stems from chronic homelessness, racialization, or learning disabilities is being looked at with a critical eye in what some people are terming "the great awakening." This term is a neologism that comes from the word "woke," meaning awake to or aware of the social injustices that occur as a result of modernization, white supremacy, misogyny, and ableism in society.

Children in the future may have a firmer grasp on the failings of government and public systems, having been raised in a time where these failings are under high public scrutiny. Many caregivers and parents take their children to protests, wearing the appropriate safety gear (masks, gloves, etc). The goal with addressing mental health issues is to give people the tools to cope with their realties, or the tools to effect change in reality so as to be able to live in a world with which one can cope. Future children will have the tools to address systemic racism far better than the generations before them, due at least in part to the by-product effect of the coronavirus. As protests about police brutality have increased, the public has begun to demand that local and federal governments divest from their police services, and reinvest in public health services such as counselling, sheltering, and family planning. By all accounts, it looks as though the trauma of a global epidemic that has seen the death of thousands of humans world-wide may have a series of positive offshoots for the next generation.

Chapter 6:
Final Thoughts

In this chapter we have discussed the hygiene, nutrition, cognitive wellbeing, and mental health of young children as those things relate to the ongoing event of the coronavirus pandemic. Suffice it to say that the quiet truth of these matters of childcare is that they all too often fall onto the metaphorical plate of female caregivers, even when those caregivers are also full-time income earners in the household. Children need many levels of care, and they are developing attitudes about their loved ones and about the world around them generally. It is important to nourish young minds with love, affection, pride in accomplishments, understanding and guidance in missteps.

It is equally important for caregivers to create an example for the children in their lives that they would be proud to point to and show to society. This is especially true in terms of gender roles. Because gender roles are a social construct, these behaviours are learned from an early age by the modelled behaviour of caregivers, even if there is only one caregiver in the house. If young boys and girls are shown that women are submissive to housework and other forms of domestic labour, they will grow to believe that the role of women is to perform that labour, and they will never even realize, perhaps until they are much older, that it was something that they learned at all.

If young boys and girls learn early on that the division of domestic labour is split equally among all members of the household, regardless of gender, they are likely to expect this to be true of their partners later in life, and less likely to accept gender inequality in other areas of their lives, including the job market. It's vital to remember that as a caregiver, you are not only helping to shape the immediate environment of the child in your care, but also their worldview and the resultant behaviour that they will grow into as an adult member of society. The spoken and unspoken biases against members of other genders, sexes, colours and creeds can stop in a generation with the appropriate discussions and education. The language of understanding can change from a clunky pidgin to a flowing creole.

Section Three:
Caring for Seniors

Chapter 7:
Introduction

In this section, we'll discuss caregiving methods targeting the second group of dependents in Canada: senior citizens. Seniors in Canada are a rapidly growing segment of the population and are living longer and healthier lives than previous generations (GC, 2014). Senior care is a necessity for millions of Canadians, and that need is expected to do nothing but grow in years to come. In 2014 there were over 6 million Canadians aged 65 and older (GC). By 2036 this number may double, potentially outnumbering children, a historical first (Statistics Canada, 2009) with seniors making up approximately 25 percent of the population. Increased life expectancy rates also contribute to the percentage growth, as life expectancy in Canada, The United States, Sweden, Australia, Japan, France, and the United Kingdom has increased by thirty years in this century (Brody et al., 2000).

These statistics are highly indicative of the future demand for unpaid caregivers and the importance of growing our knowledge and understanding of the caregiver experience (Canadian Institute for Health Information, 2018). Many individuals have turned to senior retirement homes for this needed care, but there are options potentially more appealing for individuals who wish to remain in their homes. Informal caregivers—family and friends who provide unpaid assistance with tasks such as transportation and household duties, and personal care—help seniors remain in their homes, thereby reducing demands on the health care system (Statistics Canada, 2012).

Challenges faced by seniors requiring care often vary depending on age and mobility. Some seniors are fully able to move around, run errands, and tend to their own personal care. Others require assistance getting from place to place, as well as with cooking, household and personal care. The greater the complexity of the senior's needs, the greater likelihood that caregiving responsibilities will be more demanding and require more time spent with the senior in care. All that is required to provide care is dependent on the senior at hand, the living situation, and the caregiver. No two caregiving situations are identical.

Maintaining happiness and a positive outlook on life can become challenging for some seniors, as loss of spouses, altering living circumstances, and loss of energy can have a negative impact on happiness levels. This is also often the case with individuals experiencing compounding disadvantages that limit the ability to care for oneself, tying into an intersectional framework. There can also emerge the feeling of being left out or forgotten, as the world continues to progress, and the lives of seniors often tend to slow development or change infrequently. As technology advances, it is common for elderly individuals to face difficulty adapting to these advancements.

Though we regularly come across remarkably bright older individuals, there can be situations where even they cannot steer clear of some of the setbacks associated with the use of information and communication technology, as well as the psychological demands of learning - that for them - is something entirely alien and new (Vacek & Rybenska, 2016). Seniors, like other individuals, while being at ease in a group and communicating easily with each other, may be shy when it comes to asking a question lest they see themselves appearing to be incompetent or not well informed. However, as seniors age, physical and mental stimulation through in-person contact is an essential part of care, and tactical measures can be taken to encourage individuals to try new things, or stimulate their minds in other ways. This was also a different process prior to the COVID-19 pandemic, but the need remains as vital as it has always been.

A Canadian technically becomes a senior at 65, but seniors often do not require care until years later. Only one quarter (27 percent) of individuals receiving care were in their mid-70s, with nearly half of this group aged 85 years and above (Statistics Canada, 2012). This poses the question: who takes care of seniors at home? The level of care required varies depending on the number of tasks a caregiver is expected to regularly perform. Individuals desiring at-home care require a variety of services such as transportation, house cleaning, cooking, financial management, and assistance with personal care.

As mentioned, seniors have viable options for caregiving, two of the most popular choices being retirement homes and at-home care. Beyond reducing demands on the health care system, there are many other reasons why a senior may choose at-home care. Remaining in one's home can provide a feeling of comfortability, while also leaving some sense of independence and ability to navigate on one's own. A home can also act as a reminder of other significant aspects of life such as family and past memories. According to a poll conducted in October of 2011, 52 percent of baby boomers said they were unlikely to move someplace new in retirement. In a 2005 survey by AARP, 89 percent of people aged 50 and older said they would prefer to remain in their home indefinitely as they age (Verona, 2011).

Luckily, there are options for receiving care at home, but depending on financial security, hiring formal at-home care can be unrealistic. According to the 2008/2009 Canadian Community Health Survey, an estimated 3.8 million Canadians who were aged 45 or older (35 percent) were providing informal care to a senior with a short- or long-term health condition. Women made up 57 percent of these Canadians (Statistics Canada, 2012). This responsibility is regularly taken on by the individual's offspring, making the role slightly less traditional or gender selective. However, it is common for the individual who holds the majority of domestic responsibility, such as a stay at home parent, to take on the role of caretaker. As reported in the introductory section describing traditional gender roles, these responsibilities are still mainly taken on by women.

Half of all caregivers (47 percent) reported caring primarily for their parents or parents-in-law (Statistics Canada, 2018), making this the most common form of caregiving reported, particularly common among caregivers aged 45 to 64. This means there are many individuals who will act as caregivers to seniors while they are seniors themselves. Depending on the caregiver's age, the ability to provide full time at-home care to a senior can be challenging, especially when experiencing the global spread of COVID-19. In order to provide the best level of care during this time, caregivers must be able to establish a balance between their work and their own self-care.

In light of the pandemic, remaining in one's own home may be a more viable option for some seniors. However, social isolation among older adults is a serious public health concern because of their heightened risk of cardiovascular, autoimmune, neurocognitive, and mental health problems (Lancet Public Health, 2020). Those responsible for at-home care will face new challenges, as caregiving while physical distancing means less access to external services and more responsibilities for the caregiver (GC, 2020). With these new challenges comes pressure, as seniors are some of the most vulnerable to the virus. The early death cases of COVID-19 outbreak occurred primarily in elderly people, possibly due to a weak immune system that permits faster progression of viral infection (Rothan & Byraredy, 2020). This has resulted in the majority of COVID-19 related deaths occurring within the elderly population; eight out of ten deaths caused by the virus have been seniors (Centers for Disease Control and Prevention [CDC], 2020).

Putting effort and attention towards senior care throughout and following the pandemic is incredibly important. If health ministers instruct elderly people to remain home, have groceries and vital medications delivered, and avoid social contact with family and friends, urgent action is needed to mitigate the mental and physical health consequences (Lancet Public Health, 2020). With loneliness, social disconnectedness, and the chance of coming into contact with a potentially life-threatening disease, stress is inevitable. Irritability, depression, anxiety, and other indicators of mental health can be affected by changes in environmental quality (Evans, 1982). The uncertainty of when circumstances will return to a normal that allows senior contact with others, leaves additional stress.

This section highlights common difficulties faced by seniors before, during, and following the peak of the Coronavirus pandemic, focusing on difficulties faced by caregivers, finding the balance between senior care and self-care, and navigating through these times maintaining the most beneficial impact for seniors and caregivers. Senior care during this time becomes an immense responsibility, and caregivers must pay close attention to caregiving methods, as well as their own personal actions and day-to-day lives. It is worthwhile to consider both the short-term and long-lasting changes that will be required to ensure prevention of COVID-19's spread to seniors.

As our world works to determine the long-lasting impact of the COVID-19 pandemic and the level of necessary cautionary measures needed, the elderly will likely face the longest lasting, highest level of these measures, as they are most susceptible. This section explores in detail all that is required of an at-home caregiver for seniors, highlighting job requirements prior to the pandemic, how the job has changed since the global spread of the virus, and drawing evidence to predict how the job will be changed following the virus' peak.

Provinces began initial reopening phases in May of 2020, with the second and third phases not far behind, but the same lessening of regulation can't be expected for seniors, who are the most susceptible to the virus. It is no surprise that the expected responsibilities of at-home caregivers have increased and have altered to accommodate the standards required in an attempt to flatten the curve. As social distancing transitions between societal regulation and a suggestion, at times it can be difficult to know where the line is. However, caregivers must practice extra levels of caution, as they are not only responsible for their own health, but the health of the individual(s) in their care. Focus will be drawn to specific tasks regarding transportation, household and personal care, implementation of a social life, physical and mental stimulation. Another large area of focus will be on mental health, factors affecting quality of life for seniors, and the assistance in adapting to change.

Chapter 8:

Before the Pandemic

As individuals age and become more dependent on care from external sources, the type of needed care increases in variety. This was true before the spread of COVID-19 and in this case, the pandemic has not lessened the caregiving workload. Scripps Gerontology Center at Miami University defines care as ADL (Activities of Daily Living) assistance, whereas support is considered to be all other assistance, such as financial help, material resources, and home modifications (McGrew et al., 2017). Statistics Canada (2012) reports transportation as the most common form of care provided prior to the Coronavirus spread, reported by 39 percent of caregivers. About 20 percent were assisting with household activities, and around 15 percent with personal care (Statistics Canada, 2012). Additional responsibilities include physical and mental stimulation, participation in a social life, assistance with the constant changes to our technological and societal world, and helping to maintain happiness and quality of life.

A slight majority (56 percent) of care receivers are women, partly reflecting longer life expectancies and corresponding greater representation as seniors (Statistics Canada, 2012). When determining reasons for care, a number of gender differences were evident but explained by age-related illnesses and gender-specific health conditions. Women were more likely than men to receive care for aging needs and arthritis, both relating to the greater number of senior women. Family and friends are recorded as the most common source of at-home care and support.

Focusing on challenges faced by caregivers of senior citizens allows for a greater analysis of the job and the physical and mental tolls it takes. It is also important to recognize both the positive and negative aspects of the experience to establish a more well-rounded view. Though senior caregiving is often a required responsibility for children, in most cases it is a responsibility taken on without a second thought, especially if families are not financially able to provide formal care. Caregivers report that they do not necessarily have an understanding of the undertaking or the time they are committing to, but rather that the role evolves and emerges (Lee, 2009). Offspring acting as caregivers record receiving a sense of fulfillment knowing they were responsible for providing care to elderly relatives, especially parents.

If a family member works from home, is a stay-at-home parent, etc., this individual is likely to take on a higher percentage of caregiving responsibilities. The ability of many older adults to remain at home with a chronic illness or disability is especially dependent on a "primary" family caregiver (McGrew et al., 2017). These individuals are more likely to be women, who make up 57 percent of these Canadians caring for a senior at home (Statistics Canada, 2012). The fact that a higher percentage of caretakers have been women offers a glimpse of intersectionality; women would often take on the responsibility of caretaker regardless of personal preference or relation to the senior. Though the percentage of male caregivers does not differ greatly from female caregivers, women are reported to dedicate almost twice as much time to their tasks - 29.6 hours per month, compared to 16.1 hours for men (Statistics Canada, 2012). A main reason for the disparity in care-hours is due to the nature of tasks women have generally performed. However, depending on the proximity of the elderly individual to other family members, as well as the amount of required needs, responsibilities could easily be shared.

Prior to the spread of COVID-19, caregiving could more easily be divided and taken on by multiple caregivers, as passing the virus was not a concern. Not only this, but multiple family members could also feel more comfortable coming into contact with the elderly family member. This made the caregiving process before the pandemic a different type of job with different levels of responsibility, physical workload, and mental labour. To an extent, seniors could better maintain their own responsibility for physical and mental stimulation, as they were able to take their own approaches that often differed from younger individuals. Arranging outings and visits with friends was more easily achievable by the senior before social distancing measures were put in place. These outings could include any outdoor activity, such as going for walks, gardening, joining social clubs and volunteering, attending religious services, spending time and playing games with friends. Depending on the level of needed care, the senior in care may have been able to arrange any of these activities. However, they may be unable to get there on their own.

Transportation as senior care can be time consuming and include costs like gas and other forms of vehicle care. Luckily, many cities and towns offer transportation networks to take older people on outings such as shopping trips and medical appointments. Transportation can also still fall under the responsibility of the senior, if the senior is physically and mentally able to drive. However, approximately eight out of ten caregivers assist their seniors with transportation needs (Statistics Canada, 2009). If caregivers are responsible for all transportation, this means they must be able to arrange their schedule to accommodate the schedule of the senior first. Nonetheless, some form of transportation as care is often necessary. Though this can be time consuming and involve costs and accommodation on the caregiver's behalf, it is also a fairly easy task. As long as the caregiver has a valid license, safe and cautious driving experience, consistent awareness and practice of safety, driving a senior is similar to driving oneself.

Household care, on the other hand, meets the senior's requests and may be instructed by the senior directly. Common household duties include vacuuming, dusting, sanitation, cooking, washing dishes, laundry, and general organization. There may also likely be additional or more specific duties depending on the situation. Household duties represent a fair percentage or caregiver labour, and 20 percent of caregivers report household activities as their main focus (Statistics Canada, 2012).

Caregivers can spend hours taking care of daily household responsibilities, especially if the senior is unable to participate in many of these tasks. This can take a toll on caregivers' physical comfort and exhaustion levels, as household duties often require tedious work that requires caregivers to be on their feet. Though 57 percent of caregivers described their provision of care as "regular," this was a daily responsibility for 21 percent of them; 36 percent provided regular care once a week, once a month, or less than once a month (Statistics Canada, 2012).

When considering required duties and level of responsibility, persoal care is quite relative to the senior, especially in comparison to transportation and personal care. Necessary duties can range from ensuring seniors take their medication, to bathing and lavatory assistance. This set of responsibilities can require a strong sense of trust between the senior and the caregiver, as they can potentially leave the senior in a vulnerable state. Those who received medical or personal care, both of which are associated with greater dependency, were more likely to have received at least one other type of care (Statistics Canada, 2009).

It is also recorded that women are more likely to provide forms of personal care to seniors. With medically related tasks, women were more likely to provide assistance associated with the senior's health compared with other tasks; one in four (25 percent) female caregivers did so (Statistics Canada, 2009). The same applies to care management, making 42 percent versus 33 percent by men (Statistics Canada, 2009). Before the COVID-19 pandemic, consistent physical and mental stimulation was achievable and less of a concern for caregivers. However, it has always been necessary for caregivers to ensure this stimulation is taking place. Light exercise is very important for physical stimulation. However, it's important that seniors in care not push themselves, and are at least somewhat supervised while performing even slightly strenuous activity.

As mentioned, the caregiver experience varies between situations, but often faces the same general challenges. A study in Pennsylvania conducted interviews with over 200 caregivers of elderly relatives to find higher levels of stressors associated with three dimensions of caregiver health: poorer self-reported health, negative health behaviors, and greater use of health care services (Son et al., 2007). The study reports that caregiving stress can result in changes in health behaviors exercised by caregivers to benefit their own health and well-being, especially if caregiving is full-time. Caregivers of people with greater numbers of behavior problems rate their health more poorly, take poorer care of themselves, and spend more money on their health care (Son et al., 2007). Challenges increase in severity depending on the level of needed care for each individual, relative to the elderly individual at hand and the intersectional factors requiring assistance. Tasks may be as simple as dropping off groceries and assisting with household care, to full time work ensuring individuals are washed, dressed, and fed. Adding financial burdens to this balance increases the potential for stress, especially for informal caregivers who are not receiving any form of compensation for their care.

Even prior to the pandemic, not all individuals were able to afford formal care, creating a need for informal caregiving. Many caregivers require some form of social or financial support, as the workload can negatively impact stress, physical and mental health, and financial burdens. Support to caregivers can take several forms, including unpaid assistance provided by friends, neighbours and families, as well as paid services and assistance received from government programs and tax credits. In 2018, about 70 percent of caregivers said they received some kind of support or assistance for their caregiving duties (Statistics Canada, 2018). This is often very useful, as caregivers are required to take on a growing list of tasks to ensure the senior in care is healthy, clean, relatively active, and able to accomplish the individual tasks required of them, whether that be on their own or with assistance.

If social support is needed, caregivers can join provincial caregiver support programs. The Government of Alberta provides one such program through work with Caregivers Alberta, an organization focusing on caregivers as individuals and helping them maintain their well-being. Caregivers Alberta offers group and one-on-one support to help caregivers connect and navigate the system, while also working to increase community support through education and networking, and advocating for policy changes that will positively impact caregivers (Caregivers Alberta, 2019).

The Canadian Government offers different forms of support for seniors themselves, which, depending on the situation and relation of the caregiver to the senior, can potentially lessen the financial load. The National Seniors Council advises the government matters related to seniors' well-being and quality of life. Members include seniors, representatives of seniors' organizations and experts on seniors and aging (GC, 2014). Financial security for seniors themselves is offered through programs such as the old age security pension, the guaranteed income supplement, as well as the Canada Pension Plan (GC, 2014).

There has been a drastic increase in the number of senior carers, due to an increasing life expectancy in Canada (Ysseldyk et al., 2019); this number is not expected to decrease. A study conducted by researchers at NORC at the University of Chicago (2014) predicted that over half of middle-income seniors will lack financial resources for senior housing and care by 2029, creating a greater need for informal care. With increased life expectancy rates, assuming general health is able to be maintained in the years to come, it's very likely that the informal care will be provided by a large percentage of seniors. However, depending on family situations and ability to provide care, a greater variety of unique caregiving situations may be more prevalent in years to come as the need for informal care increases.

Chapter 9:

During the Pandemic

In light of recent events involving the global spread of COVID-19, measures have been put in place to reduce the spread with the purpose of lessening the toll on the healthcare system, flattening the curve, and potentially saving many lives, especially those most susceptible to the virus. These measures include social distancing, isolation, consistent use of thorough hygiene, wearing a mask when out, and taking extra care of oneself through antioxidants, exercise, and rest. These precautions in no way guarantee immunity with the exception of complete isolation.

Throughout March and April of 2020, the greater percentage of Canadians, if they were able, worked from home and kept only in physical contact with immediate family, roommates, and other close individuals also in isolation. As Canada works to reopen provinces, these measures are slowly lessening, but the threat of the virus is still prevalent, especially for individuals with weaker immune systems. This puts many elderly people who require care at greater risk. According to Statistics Canada (2020), many seniors are dealing with worry and are concerned about their ability to navigate through the pandemic without catching the virus. Close to six in ten people aged 65 and older reported that they were very or extremely concerned about their own health, compared with 23 percent among those aged 15 to 24 and 28 percent among those aged 25 to 34 (Statistics Canada, 2020).

Added stress comes with other concerns, as maintaining a regular social life becomes somewhat of a pipe dream and is of fair concern to a great deal of the senior population. According to census data, one third of seniors live alone and may be at risk of social isolation. Since seniors are more likely to have a limited social network, lone seniors may be at risk in the context of the pandemic (Statistics Canada, 2020). However, many individuals, especially women 75 and older, stated they make regular plans to communicate with family members (Statistics Canada, 2020). This demographic is most likely to live on their own, so having the opportunity to participate in limited socialization is still likely a treat.

Another common behavior associated with this age group is that they are less likely to visit the grocery store or drugstore and are more likely to use delivery services to get essentials, but are less likely to order prepared food. If ordering delivered essentials is not a possibility, certain seniors will be reliant on help from caretakers or family members. During quarantine, elderly people who live alone or who live in a difficult situation could experience difficulty in obtaining food, drugs and other supplies (Petretto & Pilli, 2020). This is especially true for individuals who live in rural or secluded areas.

The world's altered circumstances have created situations for many Canadians that require some form of assistance, especially for elderly individuals who don't live in a central or urban area. With this extra needed care comes extra precautions. Early data from the United States show the ability of long-term care workers to spread COVID-19 between facilities where they are employed (International Long-Term Care Policy Network, 2020). In Canada, containment measures have been put in place across the provinces, including the restriction of healthcare workers to employment at a single home.

Considering the measures put in place by seniors' retirement homes can be useful for at-home caregivers when determining their new boundaries and adjustments to the practice. Luckily, at-home care decreases likelihood of contact with other seniors, but it can be difficult for at-home caregivers to isolate completely, especially in situations where delivered essentials are not a possibility. It is imperative that caregivers follow social distancing guidelines to the highest degree to avoid putting themselves and those in their care at risk, but even providing required care can put oneself in situations that risk contact with others.

At-home care may be a new experience for both a senior citizen and caregiver, as individuals consider the implications of bringing elderly loved ones home from seniors homes during this time of panic. CNN reports that conditions have deteriorated in a significant percentage of senior's centers across North America (CNN 2020). Staff shortages also have developed as caretakers become sick or are required to care for their own children at home. However, the report does not imply that at-home care is better in every circumstance, as responsibility falls solely on the family's shoulders in this case. If elderly individuals are removed from formal care centers and brought home during this global situation, it is unlikely that they could return until circumstances change, a time frame that researchers have been unable to predict thus far.

The added responsibilities that have presented themselves during the pandemic have the potential to impact the stress levels and mental health of caregivers, as they must adjust to the changes of everyday life along with additional care that must be taken to ensure seniors are not put at risk. Younger participants are recorded to be less worried about their personal health during the pandemic, and more concerned about social stressors such as family stress from confinement or putting their older loved ones at risk (Statistics Canada, 2020).

Informal caregivers are often family members, as they do not receive payment for care. These individuals must do everything they can to keep the senior in care safe, while also completing all that is required of a caregiver during a time when circumstances differ from the norm and from each other. Reasonably stocking up on necessities to avoid busy crowds, reviewing supplies for home care and personal care to ensure the senior in care can remain comfortable, and coordinating both the caretaker's and the senior's routine to the new norm can be extremely daunting, especially when circumstances change as quickly as the case of COVID-19.

Senior caregiving during the COVID-19 pandemic relates to intersectionality in the sense that if a family member decides to bring a parent into the home, the family member generally responsible for cooking and household care will likely be the individual taking on many of the responsibilities associated with the caregiving role, regardless of relation to the dependent (Statistics Canada, 2012). In regards to seniors, individuals face restrictions that, though put in place solely for safety, can feel unfair and extremely restrictive, especially as the world begins to open up again for many others. This can cause stress that has overall negative effects on health. As older adults age they may need help with being washed and dressed, cooking, and cleaning. If an aging adult develops dementia or stroke symptoms in addition to potential mobility issues, care becomes more complex, and the carer health outcomes are likely to be poorer. Adding stress and concern for well-being can increase the complexity further.

General alterations to senior caregiving assist seniors in their attempt to stay safe while remaining healthy, active, socially fulfilled, and as calm and happy as possible. Another important factor for caregiving is ensuring that seniors stay informed on the many changes happening around the world during the event of a global pandemic. During the outbreak, there is the need to share information and to spread new information in a very quick way, but elderly people could face great barriers to access information with new media, mainly due to a "digital divide" (Petretto & Pilli, 2020, p. 2). During the early stages of COVID-19's global spread, new information becomes public nearly every day, and it is important for individuals to understand the extent of impact, and the circumstances in their area.

Some caregiving alterations lessen certain responsibilities, allowing a greater opportunity to adjust and take on new responsibilities. For most caretakers, transportation has become a much smaller responsibility as individuals are advised to stay home and avoid public situations whenever possible. This is especially true for seniors. The lessened need for transport allows caretakers to focus on household care, a responsibility requiring more attention.

The Canadian Government advises consistent and thorough washing of hands, using alcohol-based hand sanitizers when unable to wash with soap and water, wearing masks when out, and avoiding touching the face (GC, 2020). Another large emphasis is placed on practicing high levels of sanitation in regard to household care. By ensuring surfaces are regularly sanitized, especially those regularly coming into contact with individuals like doorknobs, cupboard handles, and countertops, the likelihood of catching the virus at home lessens.

Personal care requires the same level of consideration and value. Ensuring the senior in care practices the best possible hygienic practices can at times at least partially fall into the caretaker's responsibilities, depending on the age and mobility of the senior. If possible, ensuring proper personal care can be done by being tested for COVID-19 in a safe setting. However, it is important to take the level of risk for the senior into consideration; if the senior in care feels healthy and has not left the home during the quarantine period, the caretaker must determine whether it is worth it to take the senior in public to be tested.

Maintaining physical and mental health is also a necessary aspect of care during the COVID-19 crisis, and can be a greater challenge due to restrictions. Ensuring both the caregiver and the senior maintain a healthy and somewhat active lifestyle can help to lessen the mental burden while also providing both individuals with more energy and likely a more positive day-to-day outlook. Mental stimulation is often considered equally as important, though more creative activities may need to come into play. Dealing with personal stress can be challenging, especially when an event such as this creates an impact.

The World Health Organization (2020) advises caregivers to maintain a routine, put daily effort towards at-home education, openly discuss feelings towards current circumstances, and dedicate time for fun planned entertaining activities, rather than simply passing time. It is important to remember that stress and feelings associated with it are by no means a reflection that you cannot do your job or are weak (WHO, 2020). During a global crisis of this proportion, mental health can be negatively impacted by many different factors. It is important for both the caretaker and those in care to put effort towards maintaining mental health. Focusing on joy and gratitude can have a positive impact on both the senior and the caretaker.

The Ontario Caregiver Organization provides an information package on maintaining mental health during the COVID-19 outbreak. General suggestions include seeking information from trusted sources, keeping a regular routine, staying connected and maintaining social networks, tending to personal needs, and finding opportunities to share positive stories and acknowledging those in your circle of care. A final suggestion is to prepare a contingency plan should the caregiver become ill and need to self-quarantine (Ontario Caregiver Organization, 2020). This saves the caregiver unnecessary stress during recovery and provides a plan for the senior in care.

If seniors seek aid during the pandemic, it is possible to apply for the Canadian Government's new COVID-19 aid for seniors. At the time of writing, there is no government set funding as aid for caregivers during COVID-19, though caregivers can still take part in support programs like Caregivers Alberta. However, support may be limited as most contact is currently still carried out online. All Canadians are able to apply for Canada's Emergency Response Benefit, and receive funding if qualified. However, this is not enough to take care of oneself as well as a senior in care. Looking ahead to determine the long-lasting impact of COVID-19 for seniors, as well as the best plan for supporting caregivers, can be difficult to predict, as society still lacks the necessary information needed to bring the spread to a halt.

Chapter 10:

After the Pandemic

At the time of writing, researchers are still unable to predict the exact worldwide outcome following the pandemic, but we can be certain that the impact will be massive and affect countries worldwide. As new cases begin to lessen across the world, many countries predict a second wave, and the timeline for the discovery of a vaccine is still unknown. This leaves society with a long-lasting impression of what the world could be for years to come. However, as countries attempt to find a safe balance between conserving the economy, keeping businesses afloat, and keeping people safe, reopening is inevitable; but this may not be the case for the elderly and other vulnerable individuals.

Considering this mass impact raises questions regarding how to sustainably care for elderly and potentially immune-compromised individuals who may be required to avoid contact for a significantly longer period. Until there is use of approved treatments for the virus, prevention is crucial. As provinces set in motion multiple phases of reopening businesses and centers, facilities like senior care homes will likely still face cautionary restrictions to a high degree, as individuals in these homes are more vulnerable. Though seniors living at home can determine their own boundaries on more of a case-by-case basis, it is likely that their restrictions will be similar to that of a senior's formal care home in order to keep these individuals safe.

In comparison to the SARS epidemic, which had a significantly smaller impact and was easier to maintain control over, seniors were also some of the most vulnerable to the virus, causing extra cautionary measures to be put in place individually and through society, to best prevent contact for elderly individuals. However, COVID-19 cannot be looked at with the same level of severity, as it is more threatening with a chance of making a greater, longer lasting worldwide impression. Many individuals across North America are already struggling to make ends meet and informal caregivers are taking on extra responsibilities without knowledge of an end-date. This is not financially sustainable if the virus leaves an impact for years following 2020, and more thorough COVID-19 aid programs for caregivers will need to be established.

In April of 2019, prior to the emergence of COVID-19, an American study conducted by researchers at NORC at the University of Chicago predicted more than half of middle-income seniors will lack financial resources for senior housing and care by 2029, creating a greater need for informal care. Under the new societal and economic circumstances caused by the virus, this number of individuals can be expected to do nothing but grow. At the time of conducting the study, researchers found that more than half (54 percent) of middle-income seniors would not have enough assets to cover projected average annual costs of $60,000 for assisted living rent and other out-of-pocket medical costs a decade from now, even if they generated equity by selling their home and committing all of their annual financial resources (Pearson, 2019). As many individuals are still unable to work and have become reliant on emergency aid, their financial resources are lessened, and the percentage of individuals lacking assets to cover assisted living is expected to increase significantly.

Not only this, but facing heightened restrictions while the rest of the world begins to return to the societal norm has the potential to negatively impact mental health. As the world has faced this crisis together, for the most part, there has been a mentality that we're "all in the same boat" and can relate to one another's difficulties. Seniors will not have this experience if they are expected to remain on lockdown, and timely mental health care programs must be developed.

Referring back to the SARS outbreak and examining methods used to maintain mental health provides examples of how we can expect to tackle these needs today. Consistent updates must continue, even as new cases begin to lower, in order to ensure everyone is still able to be informed even when people are affected differently. Secure services should be set up to provide psychological counselling using electronic devices and applications for affected patients, as well as their families and members of the public (Xiang et al., 2020). This may be challenging in some cases, as newer technology often takes elderly individuals more time and effort to grasp. However, with the right application use, patience, and effort on both ends, this is still a possibility and has the potential to contribute to mental activity and stimulation for elderly individuals.

An effort to improve circumstances for elderly individuals can be taken on by a larger group of individuals as restrictions lessen. This can be done without risking the spread of the virus, through regular phone and video calls. Interventions could simply involve more frequent telephone contact with significant others, close family and friends, voluntary organisations, or health-care professionals, or community outreach projects providing peer support throughout the enforced isolation. Beyond this, cognitive behavioural therapies could be delivered online to decrease loneliness and improve mental wellbeing (Lancet Public Health, 2020).

If seniors are expected to remain isolated as restrictions are minimized, caregivers for these individuals will also be expected to practice the same levels of caution to ensure safety for seniors in care. This will also be especially challenging, and can leave caretakers feeling greater stress and unhappiness regarding their restrictions. At the moment, we can expect extended restrictions to look a lot like what has been in place since March 2020. The Government of Canada (2020) has continuously advised caretakers to limit contact as much as possible, and only one person should be providing care. As mentioned, practicing consistent sanitation throughout the household and regularly washing hands is very important. It is also advised that people at higher risk of serious illness from COVID-19 not care for another elderly individual during this crisis, in order to avoid compromising both immune systems.

It is inevitable that COVID-19's impact will leave a lasting impression on society, but no one can predict with absolute certainty the extent of this impact. In a study conducted with the purpose of gathering a sense of what the post-covid era will look like, historical examples of societal crisis-induced shifts are referenced to make informed predictions following this pandemic's peak.

> *The Black Death, which killed 25 million to 30 million people in 14th-century Europe, is credited by some historians with ending feudalism and serfdom and ushering in the Enlightenment by shifting power to increasingly scarce labor resources. We can say without*

> *exaggeration that the plague shaped the path of European history. Consider also the impact of World War II on women's participation in the workforce,* (Reeves et al., 2020, para. 3)

Regardless of what comes from the pandemic, we can be certain that alterations will be made to day-to-day activities and errands. Community-involved initiatives to make the process easier for the elderly have the potential to make a great impact. For example, establishing a more intricate food-delivery network that caters to senior citizens allows easy access to groceries and essential items. Developing a national action plan during and following the pandemic can ensure seniors across the nation have equal access to necessary goods, opportunities to do things they enjoy, and attention to healthcare needs. The Government of Ontario has released an action plan for long-term care homes in response to COVID-19's spread featuring actions to date and planned steps moving forward. The next actions involve three major steps:

1. Aggressive testing, screening and surveillance
2. Managing outbreaks and spread of the disease
3. Growing the long-term care workforce

The action plan dives into details describing methods to carry out each step efficiently and safely, and focuses on providing liveable standards for both seniors and staff. If each province were to commit to a similar action plan for seniors receiving informal care that also places emphasis on informal caregivers, seniors could feel better accommodated and potential caregivers may be more inclined to take on responsibilities with the knowledge that they have support. Having less seniors in long-term care facilities throughout the COVID-19 pandemic decreases the likelihood of a spread throughout the home, but households must ensure that they are ready to take on the responsibility of informal senior care and take extra precautions needed to maintain the senior's health.

Though the steps mentioned above have been written with long-term care facilities in mind, the general idea of each step can be applied to situations outside of these facilities. At the time of writing, there is no form of at-home testing that can be used for individuals who do not feel comfortable going to testing centers. Developing government regulated at-home testing kits could allow seniors receiving informal care to consistently keep updated on their health status, likely allowing peace of mind for many, and allowing the nation to have a better idea of the total number of cases and where they are found.

At the time of writing, managing outbreaks and the spread of the virus can be accomplished by following the guidelines already put in place for individuals in their day-to-day lives. By practicing social distancing, maintaining proper hygiene, and taking additional common cautionary measures, the likelihood of catching and spreading the virus diminishes. In the case of informal at-home care, this responsibility is placed heavily on the caretaker and other younger members of the household, if any exist.

Growing the long-term care workforce can be done by redeploying health care workers from areas in the health sector experiencing fewer patient volumes, including hospital and home care resources (Government of Ontario, 2020). Not only this, but new professions can be created to meet the needs of individuals living in these new circumstances. Though elderly individuals may face greater restrictions and be stuck at home for extensive amounts of time, innovation can allow for new professions that provide essential services, mental and physical stimulation, lessen the caregiver's workload, provide a greater sense of community for those who do not regularly participate in online networks and a feeling of acknowledgment and attention for seniors.

Though many older individuals may not have expected to have to adjust to a "new normal" at this point in their lives, by practicing adaptation, innovation, and working as a community, Canada can work harder to ensure these individuals feel more comfortable and connected to their neighbourhoods throughout and following the pandemic.

Chapter 11:

Final Thoughts

In this section, we have discussed the many factors that contribute to informal at-home senior care. Senior needs are determined by the specific needs of individual seniors as well as common hurdles that the average senior citizen must face. Elderly lives have at times been devalued, and seniors do face cases of **ageism**. The Ontario Human Rights Commission describes ageism as reference to two concepts: a socially constructed way of thinking about older persons based on negative attitudes and stereotypes about aging, and a tendency to structure society based on an assumption that everyone is young, thereby failing to respond appropriately to the real needs of older persons (Ontario Human Rights Commission, 2019). Even if individuals do not hold any negative prejudices towards elderly individuals, there are cases of everyday accommodations set in place with only younger individuals in mind. This is especially the case for businesses that operate online or through newer software that can be more difficult for elderly individuals to grasp immediately.

The Ontario Human Right Commission (2019) also mentions that age discrimination is often not taken as seriously as other forms of discrimination, but can have a similar economic, social, and psychological impact as any other form of discrimination. Aging is very much based on individual experience and it is often difficult to generalize about the skills and abilities an older individual possesses based solely on their age, but most elderly individuals do face some form of limitation due to their age. The Supreme Court of Canada has stated that it is no longer acceptable to structure systems assuming that everyone is young and then try to accommodate those who do not fit this assumption. Age diversity existing in society should be reflected in the design of policies, programs, services, facilities and so on so physical, attitudinal and systemic barriers are not created (Ontario Human Rights Commission, 2019).

When it comes to informal caregiving, it becomes more dependent on individuals to practice awareness of any possible forms of ageism occurring at home or throughout the day-to-day lives of elderly individuals in care. As limitations faced by seniors are best discovered on a case by case basis, it is up to caregivers to take note of each elderly individual's needs, limitations, and attitudes towards different forms of assistance, to ensure seniors in care feel that their individual needs are acknowledged and met respectfully. Sometimes, this comes down to discussing these factors with the senior in care directly.

As mentioned at the beginning of this chapter, 35 percent of Canadians aged 45 and older provide informal care to a senior with a short- or long-term health condition, with women making up 57 percent of these individuals (Statistics Canada, 2012). Though the percentage of women is a majority, it is not staggeringly greater. However, this book's introductory description of gender and work reinforces that equality has not yet been achieved when it comes to labour, and more often than not, domestic responsibilities fall under the woman's responsibility. Women are more likely to work in roles that are consistent with their traditional gender roles. As this is still fairly commonplace, women are more likely to participate in unpaid labour and take on the role of caregiver in the home.

The typical Canadian stay-at-home parent, spouse, and informal caregiver has changed over the last few decades. In 1976, stay-at-home fathers accounted for approximately 1 in 70 of all Canadian families with a stay-at-home parent. By 2015, the proportion had risen to about 1 in 10 (Statistics Canada, 2015). This goes to show that much progress has been made, but statistics are still far from equal. In 2015, Alberta had the highest proportion of couple families with a stay at home parent in the country, sitting at 25 percent. The responsibility of caring for an elderly parent or family member often does not present itself until the caregiver has reached at least middle age. If women are to choose motherhood as one of their paths in life, this has the potential to limit their years to gain useful work experience and work their way up in the workplace during their twenties and thirties. If these women also feel expected to take on the caregiver role for elderly loved ones, this can take time away from their working or retired lives as well.

It is worth mentioning the limitations this analysis faces, as there are factors regarding race and ethnicity, and socioeconomic status that may also have an influence on the caregiver experience. If families are unable to pay for formal care for elderly loved ones and choose to take these responsibilities on, this affects each family's finances and lives. A study describing a snapshot of informal caregivers in Canada by members of the Department of Human Ecology at the University of Alberta in September 2001 provides more in-depth examples of how caregiver's lives are affected.

> *More than half made adjustments to their employment at an estimated cost to each employed caregiver of more than $1.2 million in lost current and future income. More than 40 percent incurred extra expenses, estimated at $30,630 per employed caregiver, because of their caring responsibilities. Men and women averaged between 3-5 hours per week on eldercare tasks; it would have taken 276,509 full time employees, at a cost of $5 - 6 billion, to replace the work of the 2.1 million Canadians who cared for seniors in 1996. Caregivers' physical, social and psychological health also were affected.* (Fast & Keating, 2001).

Taking this into consideration, lower income families or families facing forms of discrimination based on ethnicity or socioeconomic status may have no choice but to take on informal caregiving for elderly family members. This means these families will also need to pay for all required costs that come with caregiving, making the limitations that come with this responsibility even greater. Considering intersectionality and the caregiver experience for families with differing social identities, we can understand that those disadvantaged by multiple sources of oppression may be more likely to rely on informal at-home care from family members, which can contribute to a domino-like effect through financial burden and time and effort required to provide care.

Another significant note to make is that intersectionality often comes into play when determining what makes up the senior experience, as the likelihood of cognitive and mobile impairments becomes higher as individuals age. This can impact the caregiver experience as well. Those who care for someone with severe cognitive impairment are at elevated risk of experiencing caregiver stress or burden (Canada Health Reports, 2012). One of the most common cases of cognitive impairment for aging individuals is dementia. Dementia in Canada, a new digital report by the Canadian Institute for Health Information, highlights the challenges associated with caring for seniors with dementia. 45 percent of these caregivers experience distress, compared to 26 percent of caregivers for other seniors (Canadian Institute for Health Information, 2018).

Elderly care can describe a wide variety of responsibilities and each case is different. However, anyone who takes on the responsibility of informal care offers an extremely generous service to individuals who are no longer able to take on everything on their own, especially in situations where no compensation is received. As the world navigates through the Coronavirus pandemic, we create new ways of doing that accommodate our living situations and make it easier for us to maintain a state of normal, allowing our essential needs to be met while also maintaining our social needs and quality of life. We must ensure that throughout this time of innovation and adaptation, that we do not forget our parents, grandparents, and other elderly individuals. We can remember that many of us do not fully understand the limitations that come with age, especially since the spread of COVID-19. Providing accommodations to these individuals may allow for better peace of mind during this time of change, which is something we all hope for. Not only this, but keeping this understanding in our minds may remind younger individuals to reach out to the elderly loved ones on a more regular basis. Establishing a connection, even over the phone, can make an immense impact.

Section Four:
Caring for the Chronically Ill and Disabled

Chapter 12:

Introduction

In this section, we'll look at a third group of dependents in Canada: the chronically ill and disabled. Although a large percentage of domestic care work is performed by child rearing and caring for the elderley, the proportion of carers providing for disabled dependents is not insignificant. Approximately 22.3 percent of a sample population in 2017 self-reported having a disability (Statistics Canada, 2019), a dramatic increase since 2001 when only 14.6 percent of the sample population identified as disabled (2001 Participation and Activity Limitation Survey, 2002). The severity-level of these self-reported disabilities has also increased slightly over time (2001 Participation and Activity Limitation Survey, 2002; Statistics Canada, 2020-a). While this increase is undoubtedly due in part to an increase in visibility of disabled individuals, improved collection of statistical data, and reduced stigmatization, it is also largely a result of increased life expectancy rates (Chatterji et al., 2015). As the Canadian population lives longer, the likelihood of developing a disability or chronic illness at some point within the lifespan increases as well. Individuals born with a chronic illness or disability are also living longer than before due to improvements in medicine (Reppermund & Troller, 2016).

This begs the question: who is providing this care? The 2012 General Social Survey found that a staggering 8.2 million Canadians were providing informal care to family members and friends with a disability; that's 28 percent of the Canadian population (Sinha, 2013). This value too has increased over the years, a change that can be attributed to an ideological and political shift from formal caregiving within hospitals and other healthcare institutions to increased home care (Kepreotes et al., 2010). The latter often improves the quality of life of the individuals receiving the care, however, this change is not always a choice; a lack of financial resources can make formal caregiving assistance an impossibility for many. Regardless of the level of agency involved, informally caring for disabled dependents undeniably takes up a significant portion of the carer's time and energy.

This section follows the chapters on caring for children and the elderly intentionally, due to the intersectional framework it demands. Many disabled dependents are children and seniors (Statistics Canada, 2020-a), thus it is vital that the challenges for caregivers of non-disabled children and seniors are understood first. The unique challenges that caregivers of disabled dependents face are not separate from the other challenges of caregiving, but are rather compounded. Over a quarter of individuals providing care for the chronically ill and disabled are also caring for at least one non-disabled child living at home (Sinha, 2013). As these factors will influence the experiences of carers working from home, it is necessary to be aware that they are all components that come into play, oftentimes not separately, but at the same time.

In addition to keeping intersectionality at the forefront in this section, a discussion of terminology used when characterizing this category of dependents, and the assumptions behind these terms are first needed. The Public Health Agency of Canada (2013) defines **chronic diseases** as "diseases that are persistent and generally slow in progression which can be treated but not cured" (para. 1). They are also noncommunicable, meaning they cannot be passed from one person to another (except, in some cases, through genetics). Examples of chronic diseases are type 1 diabetes, Crohn's disease, cardiovascular diseases, and lung conditions such as asthma and chronic obstructive pulmonary disease (COPD). They may be present at birth or they may develop later in life due to environmental exposures.

In contrast, the World Health Organization (WHO) (n.d.) defines **disability** as an "umbrella term, covering impairments, activity limitations, and participation restrictions" (para. 1). Impairments refer to physical bodily or structural limitations, activity limitations to an individual's ability to complete an action without difficulty, and participation restrictions to the ability to participate in important life situations (WHO, n.d.). Thus, chronic diseases can almost always be classified as disabilities. Disabilities, however, are not always a chronic illness. For example, Autism Spectrum Disorders (ASDs) may be classified as a developmental disability, but not a chronic illness.

Classifying an ASD as a disability sheds light on another aspect of the term; its political and social implications. The term dis-ability places it in a dichotomy with the term "ability". It juxtaposes the "normal" with the "abnormal" (Ontario Human Rights Commission [OHRC], n.d.). This results in the stereotyping and stigmatization of disability. These individuals may be seen as a "burden" on society and experience unequal and unfair treatment (OHRC, n.d.). The problem, however, lies not with these individuals themselves but in the societal structure and environment around them. An individual with a mobility disability may struggle to access a particular building because it has been constructed with a non-disabled body in mind. Similarly, the classroom and teaching structure is not designed for a child with ADHD; it is designed for children who can sit for long periods of time without losing focus. Thus, the environment is the problem rather than the individual. This is called **ableism.**

While some individuals prefer to define themselves as chronically ill and not disabled, to improve readability, the term disability will henceforth be used to describe all individuals who fall under that umbrella term, as well as those who have chronic illnesses that make them more susceptible to COVID-19 or find that they face barriers and limitations and life due to their illness.

At the time of writing, COVID-19 is still a very new disease; as such, it is too early to make definitive statements about its communicability, severity and long-term health effects. Based on current data, in addition to being 65 years of age or older, individuals of all ages with certain underlying health conditions are believed to be at high-risk of experiencing severe and potentially life-threatening symptoms of COVID-19 (CDC, n.d.-a). The CDC (n.d.-a) includes the following chronic diseases in their list of applicable underlying health conditions: chronic lung disease, severe asthma, serious heart conditions, immunocompromisation, severe obesity, diabetes, chronic kidney disease requiring dialysis, and liver disease.

While having a disability does not inherently increase one's level of risk, a disabled adult is three times as likely to have cancer (and therefore be immunocompromised through chemotherapy), diabetes or heart disease when compared to an adult without a disability (CDC, n.d.-b). Although being disabled does not necessarily increase one's severity risk, it does increase one's risk of becoming infected with COVID-19. An individual with mobility and developmental disabilities may need to be in close physical contact with their carer, be unable to practice preventative measures, or have an inability to communicate any symptoms they may be experiencing (CDC, n.d.-b). Thus, health compromised individuals, who are already a vulnerable group, are likely to be particularly vulnerable to COVID-19.

Apart from the physical health concerns, a perceived - real or otherwise - risk of infection may accelerate poor mental health in disabled individuals, as well as within their informal caregivers. Preliminary studies on the psychological impacts of the COVID-19 pandemic, particularly as a result of social isolation and lockdown policies, have indicated that although the risk of infection is lowered by these preventative measures, feelings of anxiety and despair within the population practicing these measures are considerably heightened (Mucci et al., 2020). It is important to stress that it is not only the disease itself that has health impacts, but also simply the way individuals perceive the disease; these perceptions can have very real effects on physical health.

While this book focuses on the impacts of the pandemic in the Canadian context, some international research has been included in circumstances where it has been deemed applicable to the Canadian experience. In Canada, the most recent statistical data on disability are collected through the Canadian Survey on Disability (CSD). Data that follow in this chapter were obtained from the 2017 CSD and the 2012 General Social Survey (GSS); in all cases, the most up to date data were used for the primary analysis. It is important to note that Indigenous individuals living on a reserve, those living on Canadian Armed Forces bases, and children under the age of 15 were not included in the survey (Statistics Canada, 2018). This is a clear limitation of the survey and efforts to collect data on these populations is essential for future surveys.

Despite obvious limitations, valuable data have been collected. As mentioned, the 2017 CSD found that a staggering 22.3 percent (roughly 6.2 million) of the sample population self-identified as disabled (Statistics Canada, 2018). The likelihood of becoming disabled increases with age and the percentage of disabled individuals that identified as female was greater than male within every age category (Statistics Canada, 2018). This gendered difference was also evident when it came to the severity of the disability; men identified as having a greater percentage of mild to moderate disabilities, while a greater percentage of women classified their disabilities as severe to very severe (Statistics Canada, 2020-a). The type of disability was also reported and respondents could pick multiple categories for their disability (i.e. pain-related as well as mobility-related). To narrow our focus here, only values for the most general and encompassing categories are included in this analysis; 65.0 percent of disabilities were reported as being pain-related, 42.8 percent mobility-related and 32.5 percent mental health-related (Statistics Canada, 2020-b).

Another dimension of the CSD and GSS worth looking at is the income data for chronically ill and disabled adults. Poverty tends to exacerbate the effects of - or even result in - disability, and vice versa. In 2017, one-third of disabled adults reported earning under $20,000 per year and nearly half earned under $30,000 per year (Statistics Canada, 2020-c). While this number is down from the 45.3 percent who earned less than $20,000 per year in 2012 (Statistics Canada, 2020-d), it still paints a bleak picture. Additionally, only a little over a third reported receiving benefits such as the Old Age Security Pension and the Guaranteed Income Supplement (Statistics Canada, 2020-e). It is not clear whether more have applied for benefits and been deemed ineligible, or whether they have not applied at all. The economic repercussions of a social structure designed around able-bodied individuals becomes plain.

Statistical data on the informal caregivers of disabled individuals is also revealing. Of the 28 percent of Canadians providing informal care, over half identified as female (Statistics Canada, 2019). As discussed at the beginning of this book, caring continues to chiefly fall under the purview of women, despite an increase in the number of women participating in the labour force outside of the home. The type of work these carers considered to be their "main activity" also reveals gender inequality (Statistics Canada, 2016-a). Only 56.5 percent of female carers considered paid work to be their main activity, while that figure was 68.0 percent for male caregivers (Statistics Canada, 2016-a). Thus, male caregivers are likely contributing less time per week towards informal caregiving than female caregivers, subsequently allowing them to spend more hours in paid labour activities outside of the domestic sphere.

How are these informal carers related to their dependents, and how much time do they spend caregiving? Most are providing care for a parent or parent-in-law, at 48.1 percent of all informal caregivers (Statistics

Canada, 2016-b). 13.5 percent are caring for either a spouse or a child, and 22.4 percent are caring for a family member that is not part of the immediate family (Statistics Canada, 2016-b). 13.3 percent care for individuals that are not relations; this might include friends, neighbours and colleagues (Statistics Canada, 2016-b). Gendered differences make yet another appearance in terms of hours spent caring. Women were more likely to spend over ten hours each week; this was even true for women whose main activity was engaging in paid labour (Statistics Canada, 2014-a; Statistics Canada, 2014-b). The number of hours spent caring also increased with the age of the carer (Statistics Canada, 2014-a).

Differences according to gender, age and complexity of role will prove to be significant dimensions of the caregiver experience and therefore of their experience working from home with disabled dependents before, during and after the pandemic. As you proceed through the following chapters in this section, keep these three elements in mind.

Chapter 13:

Before the Pandemic

In the decades leading up to the COVID-19 pandemic, caregiving for the disabled and chronically ill had been increasingly shifting from formal care within public institutions (such as hospitals and long term care facilities) to informal care within the homes of family and friends of the recipient (Kepreotes et al., 2010). As the prevalence of homecare rose, so too did the body of research on the health impacts of informal caregiving. To understand the changes the pandemic has had on the lives of caregivers working from home with disabled dependents, two elements of caregiving leading up to this event must be discussed: the challenges caregivers have historically faced when caring for dependents (inclusive of children, adults and aging adults) with physical and mental health-related disabilities, as well as their experience of work, both within and beyond the domestic sphere, while simultaneously providing informal care.

This analysis requires that a heavy emphasis be placed on exploring the challenges faced by caregivers of disabled individuals. While the goal is to bring light to the trials these informal caregivers face in the hope that solutions might be found, it is important to recognize that, like any human experience, the act of caregiving is a nuanced experience and does not fit perfectly into clear cut categories of either "positive" or "negative". Although this analysis will primarily focus on the negative aspects, some time must first be spent in a brief discussion of the positive impacts that caregiving has on a person's quality of life. Much contemporary literature emphasizes the "burden" of caregiving, and while this sense of burden is undoubtedly very real for many caregivers, it provides an incomplete picture.

A recently-published American survey found that 83 percent of caregivers described multiple positive feelings about their role (National Opinion Research Center, 2014). Respondents in this survey frequently expressed that caregiving gave them a sincere sense of purpose, a deep satisfaction knowing they were giving back to a loved one, and comfort in the reassurance that their loved one was receiving quality care (American Psychological Association [APA], 2011). While caregiving is not easy, many carers actively choose to perform their duties; this choice is intrinsically motivated. Consistently referring to the disabled as "burdensome" perpetuates the stigma that these individuals are at best, an inconvenience, and at worst, undesirable and unworthy members of society and the economic sphere. As previously discussed, the issue lies not in these individuals but within the structure of our society and economy. Likewise, the challenges faced by caregivers are a product of the societal structure; they are not inherent to caregiving for disabled individuals, but rather the societal supports (or lack thereof) that are in place create the challenges.

These challenges themselves are varied and often dependent on the type of disability of the recipient, as well as the severity and therefore the level of need. The greater the complexity of the recipient's needs, the greater the likelihood that the carer will find their caring duties more challenging. Fairfax et al. (2019) studied the impact of caregiving for chronically ill children and found that a greater caregiving complexity resulted in poorer well-being of the caregiver (who was, in most cases, the mother rather than the father of the disabled child). They used the term **caregiving complexity** to describe "the impact of the clinical or medical severity of the child's disease as well as the social, time, and economic implications of caregiving, which may vary according to child, parent, family, and environmental circumstances" (Fairfax et al., 2019, para. 2). While this term is used to describe the experience of carers with disabled children, it can be applied to all forms of caregiving; no two carers will have an identical experience.

The concept of caregiving complexity ties in nicely with an intersectional framework. The challenges involved in child rearing are compounded when that child also has a disability. If that child has multiple disabilities, the challenges are further intensified. Similarly, caring for an aging adult has its challenges; they may need help being washed and dressed, and their cooking and cleaning may need to be done for them as well. However, adults caring for a parent or parent-in-law generally have the most positive carer health outcomes out of all types of caregiving (Ysseldyk, 2019). Conversely, if that aging adult has (in addition to mobility issues that come with age) dementia or stroke symptoms, the level of care involved becomes more complex, and the carer health outcomes are likely to be poorer.

It can be helpful to look at the effects of these challenges as contributing factors to a person's **quality of life.** These effects can be categorized within four different experiential spheres: the psychological, physiological, social, and cultural (Feigin et al., 2008). In general, negative psychological outcomes of caregiving involve poor mental health, a lack of tranquility, a feeling of loss of security and low self-image, dissatisfaction with recreation time, lowered personal potential, and avoidance of showing emotional vulnerability (Feigin et al., 2008). While putting the needs of the recipient first can create feelings of validation and purpose, a sense of having lost one's own identity and purpose can also be felt.

Though psychology and physiology, or the mind and body, are often studied as a dichotomy, there is a growing body of research that explores the dialectical relationship between them. It is widely understood that poor physical health can be a direct cause of poor mental health but the opposite is also true. High levels of stress over a prolonged period of time can cause high blood sugar and insulin (hyperglycemia and hyperinsulinemia), high blood pressure, and a depressed immune system (Vitaliano et al., 2004). Vitaliano et al. (2004) found that caregivers actually took significantly more medication for physical health concerns than those without caregiving responsibilities. They also produced 23 percent more stress hormones and had a 15 percent less reactive antibody response (Vitaliano et al., 2004).

The stress response in parents, particularly mothers, of chronically ill children is significant (Barker et al., 2012). Mothers with chronically ill and disabled children experience a higher prevalence of **post-traumatic stress disorder (PTSD)** than fathers (Sanderson et al., 2013) and these types of carers were twice as likely to have depression and physical disabilities or some form of chronic illness of their own when compared to parents of children without chronic illness or disability (Brehaut et al., 2009). These symptoms are exacerbated in parents who are participating in the labour force in addition to their caregiving duties (George et al., 2008). Parents with chronically ill children have costs three times greater than that of parents with healthy children, thus finances are another area of stress for these carers (Leonard et al., 1992).

Studies also show that carers of the disabled experience greater consequences when the disability is mental health-related (Amir, 2015). Research on the effects of caring for an individual with dementia has revealed that carers of dependents with mental health-related disabilities and illnesses are faced with more numerous and extensive challenges. The time spent within the caregiving role is long, often between three and fifteen years (Vitaliano et al, 2004). The end of their caregiving role often comes with the death of their loved one, and as such they experience a process of grief throughout their experience (Vitaliano et al., 2004). Carers report feeling a lack of control and may feel that they are being stretched in multiple directions due to competing demands (Vitaliano et al., 2004). Unsurprisingly, this can lead to feelings of depression and elevated levels of stress in carers.

These negative psychological and physical effects can be substantially mitigated by strong social networks and cultural beliefs that emphasize community and family. Carers that feel they have strong social networks, and therefore more support, emotional or otherwise, often cope better and have better mental health outcomes (Feigin et al., 2008). A substantial amount of stress comes from feelings about having inadequate time to complete tasks, multiple demands pulling the carer in competing directions (for example, simultaneously balancing a full-time job, child rearing and caring duties), and concerns over being able to hold down a full-time job in order to pay for the costs of caregiving. With social support, including help from other family and friends with caregiving tasks, stress levels are significantly reduced and physical health improved, thereby improving the psychological and physiological spheres of quality of life.

When compared to other kinds of carers, carers of disabled children often find participating in the labour force outside of the home the most difficult. They are also often the carers that are most in need of an income to provide the required care. The demands and daily stressors involved in caring for a healthy child are already challenging enough; children that have additional needs exacerbate those demands. Many parents, particularly mothers, found that full-time employment outside of the home was difficult to maintain due to having to dedicate a high number of hours to care, as well as the inflexibility as to when these hours could be performed (Kim et al., 2014; George et al., 2008). Raising children with unique needs meant that for a lot of parents, working a nine-to-five job wasn't an option. Some parents faced considerable stigma at work with employers who expressed frustration when their caregiving role conflicted with their job demands, and others actually experienced job loss when the conflicts became too much (George et al., 2008). Caregivers who did work often had to work extreme hours to obtain the flexibility needed, and finding jobs that allowed them a flexible schedule meant that their job opportunities were severely limited (Hussain et al., 2018; George et al., 2008).

In recent years, research has been done specifically on young adult informal carers, categorized as being under the age of twenty-five and therefore in the formative years of their adult life. This research has shown that this group of carers has a very unique experience and as such, deserves proper attention. Adults in this stage of life have a variety of expectations and pressures placed upon them, and the decisions they make in response to these pressures have a profound effect on the trajectory and direction of their future lives (Aylward, 2009). Unfortunately, data in Canada do not isolate this group, but what we do know is that 29.8 percent of caregivers are between the ages of 15 and 34 (Statistics Canada, 2014-a). While we do not know the percentage of respondents between 15 and 25, we can infer that it is likely not insignificant. While a large proportion of young adults without caregiving responsibilities are working either full or part-time and are receiving some form of post-secondary education, young adult carers often cannot work or attend school due to conflicting demands between the work and education spheres, and the domestic sphere (Day, 2015). This severely limits their chances of being economically successful in life.

On the other end of the spectrum, there has also been a drastic increase in the number of senior carers, due majoritarily to an increasing life expectancy in Canada (Ysseldyk et al., 2019). Using data from the 2012 GSS, Ysseldyk et al. (2019) found that older caregivers (who were more likely to be female) reported lower incomes and more time spent giving informal care when compared to younger caregivers. However, feelings of loneliness and isolation were lowest within this group, although across all age groups, the positive effects of caregiving were often less than the negative impacts (including but not limited to excessive alcohol consumption and poor nutritional and exercise habits) (Ysseldyk et al., 2019). Better mental health in these carers is likely due to a lower level of stress resulting from a lack of competing demands outside of the caregiving role (Ysseldyk et al., 2019).

Chapter 14:

During the Pandemic

In many countries, Canada included, quarantine and social distancing policies have required office buildings to close and employees be sent home to work. While it is undoubtedly the right policy choice to ensure the curve is flattened and the burden on the formal healthcare system lessened, this change has been difficult for many. Prior to the pandemic, a large proportion of childcare for many disabled and children occurs within the classroom; being at home with these children all day, seven days a week, has shifted the entirety of the care burden onto these parents. This may interfere with their work demands and cause added stress. Although the stress of balancing work demands and informal caregiving duties was high for parents before COVID-19, the chance to leave the home and go to work, thereby relinquishing care duties for a few hours, was also a welcome break (George et al., 2008). Jessica Moran, the mother of an austistic daughter, described the intensification of her caregiving role during COVID-19:

> *Community and support is the biggest part to making having a special needs child manageable. Given we have zero [outside] support right now due to COVID-19, and we are tasked through not only working through our child's special needs, emotional and mental well-being but also schooling ... it's really, frankly, near impossible.* (Schuck, 2020, para. 4).

For other caregivers of disabled dependents requiring extensive care, the move from participating in the labour force outside of the home to working within the home hasn't resulted in a massive lifestyle change. The level of care required for many disabled and chronically ill dependents means that their caregiving and employee roles are often in conflict. Many of these carers either did not work at all before the pandemic, worked from home, or worked on a more flexible schedule that differed from the standard nine-to-five workday. The societal shift from employment from the workplace to the home has meant that all employers and employees have had to become more flexible about work. This shift may be hugely beneficial to the labour force participation of caregivers of children and other disabled dependents, as they are no longer confined to a nine-to-five work day and may arrange their hours around the needs of their dependents. Finding appropriate childcare was also a challenge for many parents due to limited availability of services for children requiring specialized care in addition to the cost (George et al., 2008). During COVID-19, childcare, as well as other types of formal care no longer need to be arranged, thereby reducing the costs involved.

Although working from home during COVID-19 has helped bridge the gap between the domestic and work spheres in many ways, the most profound impact of working from home with health-compromised dependents lies in the psychological impacts of the societal shift. As discussed last chapter, negative psychological impacts of caregiving were best mitigated in individuals that stated they had social support. Family and friends provide invaluable support to caregivers, allowing them to properly cope (Taanila et al., 2002), but social isolation measures are undoubtedly restricting the benefits of social support networks. Carer Erika Moyer stressed how the pandemic revealed how much she relies on community to cope with caregiving duties:

> *Community always matters more than anything within the special needs world. At times like these, when part or all of your supports come crumbling down, you realize what a fragile structure you regularly lean on.* (Schuck, 2020, para. 13).

There is also a reduced ability to involve disabled dependents in social activities and treatments outside of the home (Lin et al., 2008); this may have negative effects on the mental health of dependents, which may thereby negatively impact the mental health of their caregivers as well. Jessica Moran's austistic daughter was so anxious about the pandemic and drastic change in routine that she wasn't able to sleep, thereby making her "absolutely unreasonable to deal with during the day" (Schuck, 2020, para. 5). To cope, she takes the day "hour by hour" and has "resorted to just escaping to a hot shower to cry [at her] breaking point" (Schuck, 2020, para. 5). Emma's son is suffering similarly: "He needs social interaction, he feels like walls start closing in and he is trapped. He could have a breakdown every second and we would need to go to the hospital, what would happen then?" (International Disability Alliance [IDA], 2020, para. 8).

Additionally, as the healthcare system shifts to focus on the treatment of the virus, medical treatments and services being offered for disabled individuals are being put on hold (APA, 2020). A lack of availability of personal protective equipment (PPE) means that caregivers must ration their supply for their loved one, creating fear and anxiety over the day when they run out (APA, 2020). Two American women with psychosocial disabilities attested to this. Jennifer relied on regular doctor and therapy visits, which were put on hold when a state of emergency was declared; she stated that the loss of these crucial appointments had taken a toll on her mental health (IDA, 2020). Similarly, Emma developed an infection, for which she was denied treatment while doctors focused on COVID-19 patients; she is now receiving antibiotics, but because the infection was so advanced by the time she received treatment, the recovery process is ongoing (IDA, 2020).

Studies on the impacts of quarantine on mental health have shown detrimental effects on the population overall, thus it is safe to assume that these effects are intensified in carers of dependents. Preliminary studies on the psychological impacts of COVID-19 have revealed fears about what the future holds, fear of contamination, and fear over potential personal death as well as the death of loved ones (Lorenzi, 2020). Post-traumatic stress, anger, confusion, a loss of freedom and independence, isolation and loneliness have been shown to have very real negative health effects that don't just lift at the same time as quarantine restrictions ease; they take considerable time to recover from (Brooks et al., 2020). Healthcare staff in particular have reported feeling exhaustion, anxiety, and detachment (Brooks et al., 2020); it is possible that informal caregivers may experience similar symptoms.

Social isolation and quarantine measures are likely to be taken very seriously by caregivers of disabled and dependents, who likely fear contracting COVID-19 and passing it on to the recipient of their care. Atkinson, the mother of a chronically ill child, explicitly expressed the fear she felt:

> *The thought of her battling a respiratory illness — when she has already lived through unthinkable respiratory stressors so many times*

in her short life — is the kind of stuff that makes me want to crumple in a pile of weeping emotions. (Atkinson, 2020, para. 9).

The physical isolation required to keep disabled and dependents who are at risk of suffering considerable symptoms of COVID-19 has a psychosocial aspect to it as well. In the early days of the disease spread, a problematic discourse began circling. Many individuals who saw themselves as healthy wondered why people were making such a "big deal" over COVID-19. They reasoned with themselves that they weren't going to get very sick, so why should the majority of the population disrupt their lives for the elderley and those with underlying health conditions? People die - it's simply a harsh reality of life. A black American man in a wheelchair, Dominique Alexander McPhearson, notes his own observation of this discourse:

> *Quarantine doesn't bother me as much as it seems to bother other people. After an accident left me paralyzed from the chest down, I've found ways to avoid crowds and I feel no pull to gather around others as a need for socialization. Society isolated and sectioned me off as soon as I became differently-abled.* (McPhearson, 2020, para. 2).

One can only imagine what, not only a disabled individual, but also a caregiver - who has given up countless hours of their life to ensure that their loved one is as safe and healthy as possible - would feel in response to this discourse. They are actively being told that they do not matter. They are being told that they are responsible for the disruption in the lives of those who are healthy and able-bodied.

> *...it's infuriating when other people around the nation continue to party and congregate in public spaces with no protection as if we're not in the middle of a pandemic. As if asymptomatic people can't pass the disease to scores of other people. All because they have cabin fever from being in the house. The numbers of dead bodies piling up mean nothing to these people because they'll be okay. Because they aren't a part of the high-risk groups.* (McPhearson, 2020, para. 20).

Palmer (2020), a disability advocate, asserts that this discourse is blatant ageism and ableism. Essentially, it is "open eugenics" (Palmer, 2020, para. 9).

Historically, **eugenics** was a movement to improve society by *encouraging* individuals with "desirable" traits to reproduce and *discouraging* individuals with "undesirable" traits (such as disability and chronic illness) from reproducing (Personal Genetics Education Project [pgEd], n.d.). It often went beyond discouragement; many "undesirables" were forcibly sterilized to prevent reproduction (pgEd, 2020). Thus, by adopting the attitude that health-compromised individuals aren't worth the inconveniences involved in protecting them from contracting the virus, they are being labelled as a burden on society and a clear complacency towards the loss of their lives is revealed; open eugenics.

In this circumstance, the concept of open genetics ties in well with the sociologist Giroux's concept of biopolitics of disposability. Giroux (2006) describes **biopolitics of disposability** as follows:

> *The poor, especially people of color, not only have to fend for themselves in the face of life's tragedies but are also supposed to do it without being seen by the dominant society. Excommunicated from the sphere of human concern, they have been rendered invisible, utterly disposable, and heir to that army of socially homeless that allegedly no longer existed in color-blind America.* (p. 175).

While Giroux is discussing the aftermath of Hurricane Katrina (specifically how the disaster revealed that not just the poor, but also the racialized suffered the most), this principle also explains the psychology and sociology behind the lens through which the disabled and elderley have been viewed by society during the pandemic; as economically undesirable, thus disposable. This stigma and fear of societal perception is very real for both disabled individuals and their caregivers and adds another layer to caregiving complexity. Though no studies have yet been performed specifically on vulnerability levels to COVID-19 arising from varying levels of stress, we know that having a high level of stress hormones results in a low antibody response (Vitaliano et al., 2014). Thus, the stress of caregiving, and additionally the stress of stigma, quite plausibly lower the immune systems of carers and their disabled dependents, thereby putting caregivers at a greater risk of contracting COVID-19 and passing the virus on to their dependents.

While it may not be enough, there are some additional supports in place for chronically ill and disabled individuals and their caregivers during the pandemic. The Canadian government established the COVID-19

Disability Advisory Group (CDAG), headed by experts from the disability community, to provide the health minister with live updates on systemic gaps and challenges that the disabled community experience during the pandemic and to provide advice on solutions to address these challenges (Government of Canada, 2020-a). Additional resources for dependents with a pain-related disability have been compiled under the Canadian Pain Task Force (CPTF), including educational materials, virtual support groups and counseling contacts (Government of Canada, 2020-b). Susan Herrfort, a mother of a daughter with fetal alcohol spectrum disorder (FASD), notes that one positive aspect to come out of the pandemic is the connection she has with a local Facebook group for carers of disabled dependents: "people are rising up to support each other in new and creative ways and that makes the island feeling dissipate" (Schuck, 2020, para. 13).

Chapter 15:

After the Pandemic

At the time of writing, the repercussions of the pandemic are not yet known; many countries are emerging from the first wave of the disease but are anticipating a second, and no vaccine has yet been developed, nor is there an indication of when once may become available, if ever. Therefore, the aim is to use past relevant research to make informed predictions about how the aftermath of the pandemic might affect carers of disabled dependents and the dependents themselves. In any case, the long term effects of the pandemic will not be known for decades, at which point they may be looked at retrospectively. Using studies on the aftermath of past events is vital to making effective plans for recovery, thus analyzing already published literature in a pandemic context may be useful not just to the current situation, but to other large scale events that are likely to be encountered in the coming years.

An important body of literature that can be used for this purpose is derived from an epistemology that has been developing rapidly over recent years: the sociology of disaster. Disasters are often thought of as scientific events that have nothing to do with people; in actuality, they have everything to do with people. A volcanic eruption on an uninhabited island in the middle of the ocean isn't called a disaster. However, imagine if the island were inhabited and the people living there were affected by the eruption; we would then label it a disaster. People are the key difference.

Another misconception is that disasters refer exclusively to events caused by the natural environment, such as earthquakes, floods and hurricanes. The best definition of disaster has four components (Tierney, 2007):

1. A disaster is an event with a clear beginning and an end; in other words, it is concentrated within both time and space.
2. A disaster is dangerous; it results in some of its society's members falling victim to it, and its infrastructure is often damaged in some way.
3. A disaster damages the existing social structure and prevents some or all of that society's essential activities from functioning.
4. Members of the given society will respond to the disaster event collectively.

According to this definition then, pandemic events can be categorized as disasters. While we do not yet know when the end will be, the beginning of the disaster can be assigned either to its point of emergence in Wuhan, or to the beginning of its global spread. Many health-compromised individuals around the world have died and economic and transport infrastructure has been damaged. Much of society's essential activities have been prevented from functioning due to quarantine measures and the closing of international borders. The implementation of measures by governments to reduce the spread and flatten the curve to reduce the burden on the healthcare system has been a collective response to the virus. Thus, all four conditions for a disaster have been met by the COVID-19 pandemic.

It therefore follows that research from a sociology of disaster perspective is invaluable to understanding how society prepares, responds to, and recovers from pandemics. These studies can be used to improve resiliency to such events. As the nature of the COVID-19 pandemic is quite unlike anything the world has seen before, many of the consequences of it are largely unknown, and future studies by academics will be revolutionary in understanding pandemic disasters in contemporary and future societies. Despite this, there are elements of the pandemic that we have seen before and which manifest themselves as patterns in human history. The aspects that are perhaps easiest to anticipate are the psychological effects, as lots of disaster research in the past has focused on this component of the recovery stage.

One of the first disaster studies in this area was undertaken by the American sociologist Kai Erikson. Erikson (1998) studied the psychological impacts of the 1972 Buffalo Creek flood in West Virginia, two years after the event took place. He found that a whopping 93 percent of inhabitants were still experiencing "emotional disturbance" (Erikson, 1998, p. 153). They described feelings of numbness stemming from a sense of helplessness, a loss of faith in the social order, and a belief that safety was nothing more than a mere illusion, thereby approaching both their present and their future "in a demoralized state" (Erikson, 1998, p. 154). Collectively, these feelings resulted from an overwhelming, all-encompassing sense of loss for the world they once knew.

This sense of loss described by the inhabitants of Buffalo Creek is an excellent example of the sociologist Anthony Giddens' concept of ontological security. Giddens (1990) defines **ontological security** as "the confidence that most human beings have in the continuity of their self identity and in the constancy of their social and material environments of action" (p. 92). In other words, it is the security that arises from the belief in the constancy of our societal structure and community, and therefore our identity within that community. Ontological security is disrupted when "one's physical, psychological and social environment and one's sense of personal agency" are damaged in some way (Hawkins & Maurer, 2011, p. 144).

Following this line of thought, quarantine and lockdown procedures that occurred during the COVID-19 pandemic are likely to disrupt an individual's sense of ontological security. By taking away the freedom to participate in society and instructing that an individual must remain within their home, personal agency is lost, and the social and material environments that the individual has become accustomed to relying on are dramatically altered. If Erikson's study on the inhabitants of Buffalo Creek and countless other studies on the psychological impacts of disaster are any indication, a loss of ontological security during the pandemic is likely to persist for a substantial period of time following a return to a new normal.

This post-disaster experience can be tied back into the experience of informally caring for disabled dependents after the pandemic. A loss of ontological security is likely to be felt much more acutely within these individuals, as before the pandemic, they were consciously more aware of the importance of their social and physical environment. Carers strive to improve the quality of life of their disabled dependents, by keeping them physically and mentally healthy. During the pandemic, these individuals came to the realization through isolation that their social environment was crucial to their own functioning, as well as the wellbeing of their dependent. They learned that they are largely helpless in preventing their disabled loved one from contracting new diseases; it is unknown whether COVID-19 will be around forever, but even if it is eradicated, there will always be new diseases that spread like wildfire in our globalized world. This realization disrupts their ontological security on a deeper level and severely jeopardizes their ability to feel positive about the future.

Ontological security aside, multiple studies have taken a more general approach to mental health and disaster. The majority have found that, regardless of the type of disaster, in the aftermath of the event, affected individuals had higher levels of depression, PTSD and stress disorders than those who were not affected (Norris et al., 2006; Sabucedo et al., 2009; Ursano et al., 2008; Van der Velden et al., 2006). Additionally, researchers found that the greater the threat of negative consequences arising from the event, the greater the level of trauma that the individual experienced (Lee & Blanchard, 2011). This trauma may be caused by a disrupted social support network and a loss of the economic resources on which the individual depends significantly for their livelihood (Lee & Blanchard, 2011).

Again, this can be applied directly to the experience of carers of disabled dependents, who perceive their level of risk to experiencing life-threatening symptoms of COVID-19 to be greater than a significant portion of the general population, who rely heavily on social supports, and who may both have a greater financial need to carry out caregiving duties as well as an inability to access the majority of jobs on the market due to the flexibility they require from their job.

Though much remains to be published, some predictive research has already been completed on the psychological impacts of COVID-19 post-pandemic, and some have studied the effects of past coronavirus epidemics. Mucci et al. (2020) predict that a "parallel pandemic" will arise following the COVID-19 pandemic, characterized by "acute stress disorders, post-traumatic stress disorder, emotional disturbance, sleep disorders, depressive syndromes and eventually suicides" (p. 63). As discussed in the previous chapter, individuals with a mental health-related disability may have aggravated symptoms due to the lack of resources that were available to them during the pandemic; their worsened condition will take substantial time to heal from (Mucci et al., 2020).

Although general post-disaster studies are useful to an analysis of the experience of carers of disabled dependents after COVID-19, more specific studies on the psychosocial effects of quarantine have been done in the past. A study on the effects of the Middle East Respiratory Syndrome (MERS) measured anxiety and anger levels in individuals both during and after quarantine (Jeong et al., 2016). The researchers found that the levels of these emotions had been reduced by more than half of what they were during quarantine in most individuals; however, for individuals who had a "psychiatric illness," these levels had decreased to a much lesser extent (Jeong et al., 2016).

In a study on the effect of Severe Acute Respiratory Syndrome (SARS) in Toronto, Cava et al. (2005) found that a return to normalcy took months. The amount of time within quarantine also had an effect on the mental health of individuals post-pandemic, with quarantine periods over ten days having a significant effect on post-traumatic stress symptoms (Hawryluck et al., 2004). Thus, the resiliency response in caregivers and their disabled dependents following the pandemic may be lower than that of the general population.

There is also currently significant worry about what the health of the economy will look like post-pandemic, with good reason. Long term economic impacts are largely unknown at present as the end of this disaster is not yet in sight. There are sure to be consequences arising from economic recessions that the world will likely face post-pandemic (Marazziti & Stahl, 2020). There's one thing all economists can agree on: the political and economic landscape we once knew is gone forever (Foreign Policy, 2020).

Many economists, including Joseph Stiglitz (2020), also predict that there will be a period of de-globalization; countries will place a greater emphasis on self-sufficiency to mitigate some of the economic impacts of a future pandemic. However, this change will mean that the gap between the wealthy and the poor will continue to increase (Posen, 2020). Many small businesses will not be able to reopen, thereby eliminating the jobs they once provided (Tyson, 2020). Other jobs lost will largely be those that were low-wage service jobs (Tyson, 2020). As disabled dependents are more likely to experience economic hardship and many work in jobs that provide them with an income under $30,000 per year (Statistics Canada, 2020-c), they are likely to be affected by this change, potentially bringing them and their carers further economic hardship and therefore higher levels and stress and anxiety, and poorer physical health; severe economic stress has been shown to increase the likelihood of developing health problems (Macdonald & Lang, 2014). Financial worries during quarantine has already been proved to be a significant factor of stress post-epidemic (Pellecchia et al., 2015).

Despite all the doom and gloom, there are potential improvements that might come out of the pandemic, positively affecting the work experience of carers of disabled dependents. Quarantine measures meant that many individuals were required to leave the office and work from home. While this shift was easy for some businesses, for others it posed monumental challenges. As pandemics may become a regular part of our future, there will likely be a focus on tailoring one's business practices to become more remote and flexible, in order to be better prepared for the next pandemic and to keep the economy functioning as much as possible. Tyson (2020) emphasizes that "other infrastructure will be necessary to enable the accelerating digitalization of economic activity" (para. 3).

As discussed earlier, carers of disabled dependents, particularly those who are carers of disabled children with multiple caregiving complexities, often find that the main barrier to their participation within the labour force, their wellbeing at work, and their anxiety level involved in the fear of being able to hold down a job while balancing their care work, is the inflexible demands of their position. The quarantine measures of the COVID-19 pandemic have opened employers eyes to the possibility of remote work and flexible working hours. This may work in the favour of carers, who may find their needs for flexibility within the workplace are less stigmatized and that employers are more willing to work with them to create a schedule that works around their informal caregiving hours.

This situation may be seen as the silver lining in the post-pandemic social context of carers with disabled dependents, as the negative economic and mental health impacts are certain to have a significant impact. It is imperative that this group of Canadians are at the forefront of post-pandemic Canadian policy making to mitigate these negative effects as much as possible and restore ontological security. Without these policies, the biopolitics of disposability will remain unchecked. Moving forward, Canada must strive for inclusivity and the valuing of all members of society; not just the able-bodied.

Chapter 16:

Final Thoughts

An analysis of the COVID-19 pandemic has revealed the myriad of competing and complicated challenges experienced by carers working from home with disabled dependents. At the root of these challenges are the inequalities of gender roles and ableist attitudes. An intersectional framework has been essential to the endeavor to understand their lived experience. Carers of disabled dependents are also mothers, children, employees, and sometimes dealing with a chronic illness or disability of their own.

While the emergence and spread of COVID-19 occurred on a scale unlike any the world has seen thus far, the response to its threat should not similarly be viewed as unique. Disaster sociologists assert that disasters function to life the veils covering the systemic issues within a given society (Matthewman, 2016). In other words, they reveal endemic societal problems that were previously hidden from the mainstream. The pandemic did not dramatically change the lives of carers and their disabled dependents - it merely exacerbated the struggles they were already facing.

One such struggle arises from the obvious disparity between the genders of the caregivers of disabled dependents. As women today are still expected to do the majority of the care work within the domestic sphere, despite also being expected to work part or full time, the unpaid caregiving role falls primarily to them. In the introduction of this book, we saw that participation within the labour force is still not equal for men and women today. Furthermore, recent employment data collected by Statistics Canada actually indicates that this disparity has increased during the pandemic.

In January of 2020, before the effects of the pandemic were keenly felt in Canada, 68.6 percent of men and 60.6 percent of women were participating in the labour force (a percentage point difference of 8.0) (Statistics Canada, 2020-f). For the entirety of April of 2020, most of the country was quarantined. The economy had come to an abrupt halt and most employees either lost their jobs or were required to work from home. Those employed within essential services worked longer and harder, continually exposing themselves to the virus to ensure that the bare necessities of society continued to function. During this month, labour force participation dropped to 64.2 percent for men and 55.0 percent for women (Statistics Canada, 2020-f). With a percentage point difference of 9.2, the gap between the genders had increased. In May of 2020, the first wave of COVID-19 began to subside and employment participation increased slightly. It would be logical to expect that this percentage point gap would have lessened between men and women through the recovery of the economy. Instead, it increased further; 67.0 percent of men were again participating, yet that value had only increased to 57.1 percent for women (Statistics Canada, 2020-f); a percentage point difference of 9.9. Thus, early data indicate that COVID-19 has exacerbated the effects of gender on employment.

While these data are problematic overall, they are indicative of unique challenges that may be affecting carers and their disabled dependents. It is not only the carers who are majoritarily female, but also the disabled dependents themselves (Thorne et al., 1997). As labour force participation is likely to be lower for both the carer and the care recipient, they are doubly economically disadvantaged - especially if labour force participation data during the pandemic continues along the same trajectory. Furthermore, disabled women who fit into the high-risk category for COVID-19 will not be able to return to work as soon as those who are not health compromised. With many of the lower wage service jobs being predicted to be lost forever (Tyson, 2020), disabled women are sure to feel the effects.

Hochschild & Machung's (1989) concept of the second shift is also evident in the experience of carers of disabled dependents due to it being overwhelmingly females that are involved in the care, in terms of both physical and emotional care work (McKeever, 1995; Thorne et al., 1997). Married women with children, both disabled and non-disabled, are also likely to participate in the labour force either part or full time in addition to doing the majority of the domestic work and childrearing. Thus, these women are not only working a second shift, but also a third shift. The most ideal circumstances for female carers are those of older women who have both retired from the labour force and whose children have grown up and live on their own. With these responsibilities eradicated, they are likely to feel less stress when caring for a disabled loved one. However, even these women experience a second shift; caregiving for a disabled dependent is an added responsibility to the domestic work she is expected to complete in the home, including the cleaning, grocery shopping, and cooking.

In addition to the gendered division of labour, the lifting of the veil has also revealed the consequences of living in an ableist society. In previous chapters, we saw that because certain chronically ill and disabled individuals are at a greater risk of suffering from severe COVID-19 symptoms, their own mental health, as well as the mental health of their carers, is likely to be very poor. However, the fact that quarantine measures have been implemented in Canada and across the world is encouraging. Whether these measures were put in place simply to reduce the burden on the healthcare system, or because the protection of our most vulnerable citizens is truly important, this move has undoubtedly reduced the risk for disabled dependents and their carers.

The backlash that mandatory isolation laws created is, however, less encouraging. Able-bodied, healthy individuals demanded to know why they had to stop seeing family and friends outside of their household, why the economy had to be put on hold and why they had to work from home and be denied non-essential services. This stigma was felt profoundly by carers and their disabled dependents, adding further psychological - and therefore physiological - stress. Many mental and physical health services designed to deal with the stressors that carers and their dependents regularly experience were cut as the focus was shifted to prioritizing COVID-19 treatments and preventions within the health system.

Time and time again, studies have found social supports to be crucial to the wellbeing of carers and their disabled dependents. Several online resources for carers and their disabled adult and child dependents have provided tools to help these individuals to cope during and after the pandemic. One such resource is Bridge the gApp, which provides a service directory, information on various mental health issues, activities to improve coping, and access to online programs (Bridge the gApp, n.d.).

Resources like these are invaluable, but more work needs to be done to destigmatize disability and chronic illness.

Although this section has aimed to be as thorough and encompassing as possible, clear limitations exist, due primarily to gaps in available research. Intersectional dimensions such as ethnicity, sexuality and alternative gender identities are clearly missing, despite many chronically ill and disabled dependents, as well as their carers, identifying as non-white, non-heterosexual and non-binary.

As mentioned in the beginning of this section, the data on Canadians who self-reported having a disability or chronic illness did not include members of the Indigenous community. This is problematic, as their experience is likely to differ considerably from that of the general population. On many First Nation reserves, housing is substandard (Patterson & Dyck, 2015). The presence of mold in many of these homes means that many individuals have compromised-health and respiratory conditions (Gould Soloway, n.d.). These conditions are likely to make them high risk individuals for COVID-19. Although funds are allocated to complete housing repairs, the issues are often so extensive that they make very little impact (Indigenous Corporate Training Inc., 2018). As the entire budget is often used up on repairs, no new housing is built; this is extremely problematic considering the Indigenous population is growing (Indigenous Corporate Training Inc., 2018). A lack of housing means that the housing that is available is extremely overcrowded, with several generations living within one small home. Again, having a high number of individuals per household increases the likelihood of COVID-19 spreading voraciously.

Many reserves are remotely located, and while this may be seen as a protection against COVID-19, the reality is different. Only about 20 percent of Indigenous peoples live on reserves (Statistics Canada, 2018), thus the majority are either living in small non-reserve communities or census metropolitan areas. When Indigenous individuals return to their small communities or reserves from a city where the risk of contracting COVID-19 is much greater, they may become COVID-19 carriers and spread the virus amongst the vulnerable individuals within their community. Individuals living on reserves also sometimes work in essential services off-reserve, and thus leave and return to their community on a daily basis (Skye, 2020). Near the town of High River in Alberta, an outbreak of COVID-19 occurred within the Cargill meat-packing plant

(Skye, 2020). Many of the workers were High River residents, causing the virus to spread extensively through the town. Some of the workers at this plant were also members of the Stoney Nakoda Nation and inadvertently brought the virus back to their community, where 15 individuals contracted the virus.

Furthermore, due to the remote location of reserves, access to healthcare is often very poor (Gunn, 2020). Access to services is also often a challenge for Indigenous communities due to systemic and individually-perpetuated racism (Skye, 2020). These factors, as well as countless others, are likely to create a very different experience for Indigenous carers of disabled dependents before, during, and after the COVID-19 pandemic. A study on this demographic exclusively should be conducted in the near future to improve this community's unique vulnerabilities and resiliency, as well as to continue to work to repair the ongoing legacy of colonialism in Canada.

While the Indigenous community requires substantial attention, the experience of recent immigrant carers also must be studied independently. As discussed in previous chapters, an assessment of quality of life can be divided into four components: psychological, physiological, social and cultural (Feigin et al., 2008). The cultural component will vary depending on the ethnic background of the carers. First and second generation immigrants to Canada are likely to have strong ties to their cultural background and cultural norms concerning family and care will play a big role in how these carers cope with their informal care duties. Again, to understand this demographic more accurately, studies on this group alone must be done.

It is also unclear how working from home impacts carers who are in non-heterosexual relationships and who do not identify as male or female. Queer parents with a chronically ill or disabled child or parent may find that care duties are divided up more equally between them, or they may find that they face double discrimination and stigma. Their support networks may be smaller if they've been ostracized from their families, or it may be large if they've found community in friends. Research on this demographic specifically must also be done to prevent carers with multiple intersectional oppressions from falling through the cracks.

Section Five:
Caring for Caregivers

Chapter 17:

Resources for Caregivers

Community-Based Resources for Caregivers

While arguably not enough, organizations exist across the country that provide support to caregivers of aging adults, as well as chronically ill and disabled individuals. An example of one such organization is Caregivers Alberta. They offer both in-person resources as well as online resources for carers who are unable to physically meet in person. During the COVID-19 pandemic, resources were switched entirely to virtual delivery, and many new resources were developed to specifically address unique challenges presented to caregivers as a direct result of the pandemic. Some of their virtual COVID-19 resources include an online peer support group, the ability to connect with a caregiver advisor for one-on-one support, and workshops aimed at dealing with increased levels of stress, anxiety and isolation. Other resources include writing workshops that aim to provide a creative outlet for carers, advice on setting up healthy boundaries, budgeting tips to ease financial stress, and mechanisms to cope with feelings of grief.

Organizations of a similar nature in other Canadian provinces include, but are not limited to, the following: Family Caregivers of British Columbia, Saskatoon Caregiver, Saskatchewan Brain Injury Association Caregiver Support, the C.A.R.E. Program founded by The Canadian Mental Health Association, Teva Canada, Manitoba Caregiver Coalition, Comfort Keepers Manitoba, ElderCare Edmonton, The Ontario Caregiving Association, The Ontario Caregiver Coalition, L'Appui Quebec, and Caregivers Nova Scotia. Unfortunately, there is a lack of services in some of the maritime provinces and territories, as is often the case in the more remote geographical areas of Canada.

In situations where caregivers do not have access to in-person community support, there are online support communities that they may join. While physical, face-to-face relationships cannot be replaced, having access to at least some level of connection with individuals who may share similar experiences is still undoubtedly of value. Some private support groups on Facebook that carers may request to join include the following:

1. **Caregivers Connect:** Members are composed of both formal and informal caregivers providing care for a loved one. Carers may share personal stories, and ask for and offer advice.
2. **The Caregiver Space Community:** This Facebook group is an extension of the website, TheCaregiverSpace.org. It includes magazine articles written by carers about their experience and has a penpal service that matches a carer with other carers.
3. **The Caregivers Assist Support Group:** By focusing on self-care, this group assists carers with finding a healthy balance in their lives.
4. **Working Daughter:** This group is for women who are taking care of an aging parent, while also balancing other demands of their lives such as child rearing and full or part-time careers.

Similar organizations also exist for parents of children, who experience challenges quite different than those of carers of the elderly and disabled. The YWCA runs a free program called COMPASS (Community Parent and School Support program), tailored to parents with children aged 12 and under. It targets the development of both parents and their children by teaching parenting skills (relevant specifically to their own child), as well as socializing, problem-solving, and goal-setting for the children. They also offer in-home visits and are an excellent gateway to other relevant community resources that may be a good fit for the family in question. The Canadian Pediatric Society provides an extensive list of community-based support services for parents across the country, according to the province that the parent lives in. Some resources are specifically tailored to Indigenous parents living in both urban and remote communities, who face additional challenges due to their marginalized status. Others are tailored according to the age of the child and the experience of the parents (new mothers versus experienced mothers).

As is the case with carers of chronically ill and elderly individuals, the ability to find community support in person in remote geographical locations can be a challenge, thereby making online community support groups the only option. Facebook is again a valuable resource for these individuals, and a few relevant groups are as follows:

1. **Parenting a Child with Anxiety:** A group for parents with anxious children, who need a place to vent and ask for advice.
2. **Extremely Good Parenting Hideout:** This group focuses on giving and receiving advice about answering difficult questions from children and addressing behavioural problems, as well as simply providing support through shared experiences and positive outcomes.
3. **Raising Poppies:** Members of this group are parents of "gifted" children, who often find that their experience of parenting is quite unique. The emphasis is on sharing stories and providing support when things get tough.

While the pandemic has resulted in countless acts of kindness and a strengthening of community and familial bonds in many circumstances, it has also exacerbated the effects of abusive relationships. The prevalence of domestic violence during the implementation of quarantine and lockdown policies has skyrocketed, leaving women and children more vulnerable than ever before (WHO, 2020). As the majority of carers are female, many caregivers are at risk. The WHO (2020) recommends that individuals at risk for becoming victims of domestic and sexual abuse during COVID-19 identify someone, whether it be an acquaintance, friend or family member, to whom they can go to if they need to immediately leave their home. In the case that no suitable contact exists, they should become aware of shelters in their area and have a transportation plan in place to reach that shelter. The Ending Violence Association of Canada provides an extensive list of shelters and other domestic abuse resources for each province, as well as contact information for crisis lines across the country. They also provide instructions for clearing browsing history upon leaving their website and stress that, if in immediate danger, the best course of action is to immediately call 911.

Self-Care Resources for Caregivers

Although caregiving for dependents can bring enrichment into the lives of carers in many ways, the extensive and often complicated nature of the unpaid work can have a significant negative impact on the carer's mental and physical health. The COVID-19 pandemic has, in many cases, resulted in barriers to accessing community resources such as group and personal therapy sessions, after-school programming, daycare, and group outings. Mothers and children have been exposed to increased domestic violence with few options for escape, adult children caring for their senior, health-compromised parents have experienced a loss of outside help with the care work - therefore making them the sole providers of care - and carers of disabled and chronically-ill individuals have lost their social support networks.

However, the limited number of resources available cannot be blamed entirely on the pandemic. As an abundance of studies have shown, caregivers have historically been more likely to report poor outcomes in terms of both mental and physical health. This indicates that the supports available to caregivers have not fully met their needs; the system is failing in one or more ways. While the improvement of publicly-funded community resources must be at the forefront, the likelihood of this happening to the extent that carers fundamentally need is essentially nil. In a perfect world, societies would take care of their most vulnerable and no one would fall through the cracks, but this is not reality. Until these cracks are filled, the personal agency of caregivers as creators of their own reality will remain relevant.

In Western societies, the term "self-care" is tossed around with a desensitizing casualty. Women in particular are finding they have more and more on their plate, and the increase in competing demands over the past few decades have resulted in 73 percent of Canadians reporting at least some level of stress in their lives (Crompton, 2015). Recent years have seen an increase in social media posts stressing the importance of self-care strategies to combat the pressures of living in a capitalist society in the twenty-first century. We've seen the word countless times, but what does it actually mean?

The WHO (n.d.-b) defines self-care as "the ability of individuals, families and communities to promote health, prevent disease, maintain health, and to cope with illness and disability with or without the support of a healthcare provider" (para. 1). This definition is overgeneralized; the key word in self-care is, of course, self. Said simply, it refers to an individual's agency in promoting their own physical and mental health; it is the amalgamation of factors that determine a person's level of hygiene, nutrition, lifestyle, and methods of self-medication (WHO, n.d.-b).

An individual's ability to engage in self-care practices depends on particular environmental factors, the most significant of which is their socioeconomic status (SES). The greater an individual's SES, the more likely they are to have both an excess of time and money to spend on self-care. However, as caregivers of children, the elderly, and the disabled and chronically ill are more likely than the general population to lack both time and money, the resources mentioned below strive to take into account these limitations. Moreover, caregivers are likely to have strong qualities of selflessness and altruism, they are more likely to feel guilt about taking time solely for themselves. If for no other reason, caregivers should focus on taking time for self-care not just for their own health, but because a caregiver who is healthy can perform higher quality of care work. Thus, the remainder of this chapter will focus on accessible self-care resources that caregivers can use to improve their mental and physical health, either to replace failing public health services or to supplement them.

The first form of self-care involves maintaining proper hygiene. The benefits of this act twofold: cleanliness helps prevent the spread of disease as well as contributes to a person's sense of self-esteem. By just taking fifteen minutes in the morning and before bed, carers can maintain proper dental hygiene by brushing and flossing, protect skin by cleansing, moisturizing and applying sunscreen, and use their time in the shower to remove dirt and debris from their hair. Women often face strong gendered societal expectations when it comes to styling their hair, and the time required to meet these expectations is often a lot more than carers have to spare. To keep hair as healthy and low maintenance as possible:

1. Skip dye jobs, both at the salon and at home. Colouring hair requires more maintenance and is harmful to both the hair and the scalp in the long term.
2. Use shampoos and conditioners without sulfates, drying alcohols, and silicones.
3. Ask your stylist for low-maintenance cut suggestions to limit trips to the salon and daily styling time.

Applying a deodorant or antiperspirant and a spritz of perfume after getting out of the shower in the morning can help carers feel refreshed and put together, thereby giving them a boost of confidence and making them feel more ready to tackle the day ahead. In pandemic times, when social distancing and isolation policies are in place, it can be tempting to skip showering and stay in pajamas all day. Actively choosing to ignore this temptation - for at least the majority of the time - can have a positive impact on the mental health of caregivers.

Like following proper hygiene practices, maintaining a high level of nutrition is also highly beneficial for both the body and the mind. Physical benefits of proper nutrition include increased energy levels, higher immune system functioning, improved brain function, and a reduced risk of developing certain diseases (Tufts Health Plan, n.d.). In addition to the physical benefits, cooking and learning new recipes can be a creative outlet and a chance to develop a new hobby. It is also an effective avenue for forming bonds with others; by encouraging dependents and other household members to become involved, cooking transforms from a chore to an experience capable of creating memories that will be cherished for years to come. Many families have traditional recipes, and by taking the time to cook these and pass them down to children, feelings of nostalgia and meaning arise, thereby sending feel-good hormones to the brain and improving mental health.

Individuals with a low socioeconomic status may find that the cost of fresh produce is a barrier to healthy cooking. While a bag of spaghetti noodles and a jar of tomato sauce is undoubtedly a hard price to beat, fruits and vegetables can be affordable too. Buying produce in season and planning meals around sales at the grocery store that week can help with sticking to a tight budget. There are also plenty of free, budget-friendly recipe websites available, such as Budget Bytes. This site is run by Beth, who regularly posts new recipes and includes the cost of each ingredient, as well as calculates the cost of each serving.

After nutrition, one of the best methods of self-care for the body is exercise. Movement doesn't have to be time-consuming or intensive to be effective; even a fifteen minute walk in the morning or evening can improve both mental and physical health. The cost of a gym membership is a barrier to many, but thankfully, there are many free online resources that provide exercise routines that require no equipment and little space. Fitness Blender provides body weight workouts for all levels and takes into consideration low-impact needs of individuals with joint pain.

For those with more time, practicing yoga and meditation can also improve physical health, as well as make a significant positive impact on mental health. Again, there are many free and paid classes online, and both activities require very little, if any, equipment, making them affordable. Taking the time to connect with the body and mind in a quiet environment is one of the most effective stress management tools. While many urban areas have multiple local yoga studios, memberships can be expensive, and the time required to commute to classes and attend the class itself may mean that caregivers are unable to participate in this form of practice. Adriene Mishler offers free yoga classes on her Youtube channel, Yoga With Adriene. They cater to all levels and many are specifically intended to improve mental health. Many videos are also short, making them a great option for caregivers with limited time.

To combat stress and loneliness, especially during times of pandemic isolation, downloading counselling and self-help apps can be a great resource. Headspace costs around the same price as a Netflix subscription, and they offer a month's long free trial. In light of COVID-19, they're offering a free annual membership to individuals who are unemployed. The app consists of an extensive library of meditation and mindfulness tools, including meditation for beginners, for stress and anxiety, and for sleep. The app Calm provides similar resources.

Counselling apps have also begun to increase in popularity in recent years. These apps are a great solution for those new to counselling and those who are unable to visit a therapist in person. Many also charge monthly rather than per session, making them a little more affordable for those who do not have extended healthcare coverage. The app BetterHelp matches users with counsellors according to the specific issues the user is facing. Counselling sessions are then delivered in one of four ways: exchanging messages, over the phone, or over video chat.

For caregivers with religious or spiritual beliefs, attending a church service either virtually (during pandemic times) or in person once a week can also improve mental health, as well as provide social support. Many studies have proved that having a strong social network is one of the most important aspects to the lives of the majority caregivers, and belonging to a faith community is one of the best ways to achieve this. Looking to a higher power for strength and a sense of security has been a coping mechanism for millenia.

It is also important that caregivers make an effort to carve out a little time for fun, which means different things to different people. It might mean arranging social time with friends and family, sitting down with a good book, or going on a hike. Focusing on developing healthy routines, sticking to schedules, and finding a balance between caregiver responsibilities and participating in activities that are true to the caregiver's identity are essential to practicing self-care. This is, of course, easier said than done, and will vary in feasibility depending on each caregiver's unique situation, but emphasis on taking care of caregivers in the community is essential to improving their health outcomes.

Glossary of Terms

Ableism: A perspective that devalues and discriminates against individuals living with a chronic illness or disability (Smith, n.d.). It juxtaposes disabled individuals with non-disabled individuals and comes to the conclusion that the former are abnormal and must be fixed.

Ageism: A socially constructed way of thinking about older individuals based on negative attitudes and stereotypes about aging, and a tendency to structure society based on an assumption that everyone is young, thereby failing to respond appropriately to the real needs of older persons (Ontario Human Rights Commission, 2019).

Anti-vaccination Movement: Beginning in France in 1763 and continuing through to today, the anti-vaccination movement stems from a distrust in the process of inoculation. While there was reason to distrust the safety of vaccinations in the early days of immunization due to the limited understanding of disease at the time, within the past fifteen years, celebrities have made untrue assertions that vaccinations cause autism in children (Measles & Rubella Initiative, n.d.).

Biopolitics of Disposability: A concept coined by Henry A. Giroux in 2006 in response to the disproportionate effect of Hurricane Katrina on Black people in New Orleans. It asserts that the economically disadvantaged and racially marginalized individuals in society are not only required to fend for themselves during times of disaster, but are expected to do so without bringing themselves to the attention of the non-disadvantaged. They are seen as undesirable members of society and are therefore disposable.

Caregiving Complexity: The level of complexity of a given caregiver's experience, resulting from the severity of their dependent's disease, illness or disability, combined with social factors such as the extent of the caregiver's time, social ties, and socioeconomic status (Fairfax et al., 2019).

Chronic Illness: An illness or disease that is always present and often slow to progress, for which treatment may exist, but no cure (Public Health Agency of Canada, 2013).

Cognitive Wellbeing: Distinguished from mental health, cognitive wellbeing refers to the agility of the mind in accepting and categorizing new stimuli and solving theoretical problems.

Community Immunity: Sometimes referred to as herd immunity, community immunity results when the majority of a given population are immunized against a communicable disease, thereby reducing the disease's ability to spread and protecting the community as a whole (National Institute of Health, 2011).

Coronavirus: A family of viruses that generally cause mild, cold-like symptoms. Three known coronaviruses in human history have been transmitted from animals to humans and caused severe symptoms and death: Middle East respiratory syndrome (MERS), severe acute respiratory syndrome (SARS), and coronavirus disease 2019 (COVID-19) (National Institute of Allergy and Infectious Diseases, 2020).

COVID-19: A type of coronavirus known as coronavirus disease 2019, which first emerged in China in late 2019. On March 11, 2020, the World Health Organization declared the spread of this disease a global pandemic.

Dialectical Thinking: Stemming from philosophy, dialectics refers to the process by which two or more opposing ideas influence each other to arrive at a conclusion.

Disability: In contrast to chronic illness, disability is an umbrella term that covers impairments, activity limitations, and participation restrictions (WHO, n.d.). A chronic illness may or may not be categorized as a disability.

Embryogenesis: The formation and development of an embryo.

Epidemic: A health-related situation in which the number of cases reported of a particular disease being higher than normal for a given community (Relief Web, 2008). This term is often used in contrast to pandemic.

Eugenics: An historical movement with ongoing implications, originally intended to improve society by encouraging individuals with "desirable" traits to reproduce and discouraging individuals with "undesirable" traits to reproduce (pgEd, n.d.). This harmful practice resulted in the forcible sterilization of many individuals.

Fast-mapping: The hypothesized process by which children learn a new concept through minimal exposure. This is thought to be an important aspect of language development in children as young as two years of age.

First-wave Feminism: The first feminist movement, ocurring in the late 19th and early 20th centuries. The focus of this movement was women's suffrage, the ability for women to be able to attend school, and equal property rights for wives (Drucker, 2018).

Hygiene: The practice of maintaining a clean body and environment to prevent and eliminate the spread of disease and occurrence of illness. Intersectionality: A term coined by Kimberle Crenshaw in 1989 in response to the feminist movement that centered the experiences of white, middle-class women and was largely ignorant of the experience of Black women. It asserts that social categories, such as race, gender, sexuality, and social class should not be understood in isolation, but rather overlap and result in unique experiences of oppression (YW Boston, 2017).

Maslow's Hierarchy of Needs: A model developed by psychologist Abraham Maslow, outlining his theory that human beings have a hierarchy of needs consisting of, from bottom to top, physiological needs, the need for safety and security, social interaction, self-esteem, and self-actualization. Needs on the bottom of the pyramid must be satisfied in order for needs at the top to be pursued. (Open Text BC, n.d.).

Mental Health: In contrast to cognitive wellbeing, mental health refers to an individual's psychological level of personal comfort and to the brain's ability to cope with the unfamiliar and practical problem situations. Mental health is closely tied to physiological health, including nutrition, sleep and hygiene.

Ontological Security: A concept coined by sociologist Anthony Giddens in 1990 to describe "the confidence that most human beings have in the continuity of their self identity and in the constancy of their social and material environments of action" (p. 92). It is usually discussed in the context of a loss of ontological security, when a traumatic experience reveals that the social structure in which an individual saw as reality is in fact a mere illusion.

Overdetermination: refers to the use of a word or a concept with a single meaning to describe a separate object or idea.

Pandemic: The global spread of a new, emerging disease to which most of the population do not yet have immunity (WHO, 2010). This term is often used in contrast to epidemic.

Post-Traumatic Stress Disorder (PTSD): posttraumatic stress disorder (PTSD) is characterized by flashbacks, memory problems, insomnia, bad dreams, frightening thoughts, emotional numbness, guilt, depression, anxiety, anger, tension, and being easily startled (Lowenstein, 2018).

Quality of Life: A term referring to an individual's perception and experience of their position in the world, closely tied to their sense of satisfaction and happiness. There are four main contributing factors to a person's quality of life: their psychological health, physiological health, social network, and cultural beliefs (Feigin et al., 2008).

Second-wave Feminism: The second feminist movement occuring in the post-war period of the 1960s and 1970s. This movement sought equal social and legal rights for women, including the ability to participate full-time in the labour force (Drucker, 2018).

Second Shift: A term coined by Arlie Hochschild in 1989 to describe the unpaid domestic work that women are expected to complete on top of their full-time career in the labour force outside of the home.

Self-actualization: Refers to the personal development stage wherein an individual has realized all their goals, accepts who they are fully, and is self-aware enough to be able to recognize both their strengths and limitations (Good Therapy, 2019).

Self-care: Broadly speaking, self-care is the ability of individuals on their own, within families and within communities to take actionable and intentional steps to improve and prioritize health, to prevent disease, and to promote resilience (WHO, n.d.-b).

Separation of Spheres: Refers to the change that occurred in terms of gender and work with the emergence of the industrial age. While all work was historically completed within the home, or the domestic sphere, at this point in time men moved their work outside of the domestic sphere and into the public sphere, where they engaged in paid labour while women continued to do the unpaid labour in the home (Kimmel & Holler, 2017).

Third-wave Feminism: The third movement of feminism, occuring in the 1990s and emerging as a response to the white and heterosexual nature of second-wave feminism. It challenges the perspective that all women face discrimination equally and instead calls for an intersectional perspective that recognizes the ways in which women differ according to class, race, religion, sexuality and nationality.

Wet-nursing: Nursing another woman's baby, for reasons that are either medical or social in nature.

References

2001 Participation and Activity Limitation Survey. (2002). A profile of disability in Canada, 2001 - Tables. Statistics Canada. https://www150.statcan.gc.ca/n1/en/pub/89-579-x/89-579-x2002001-eng.pdf?st=vj2tfPCX

American Psychological Association. (2011). Positive aspects of caregiving. Retrieved May 30, 2020, from https://www.apa.org/pi/about/publications/caregivers/faq/positive-aspects

American Psychological Association. (2020, March). Advice for caregivers of children with disabilities in the era of COVID-19. Retrieved June 3, 2020, from https://www.apa.org/research/action/children-disabilities-covid-19

Amir, E. (2015). New developments for family caregivers in the context of mental health in Canada. Canadian Journal of Community Mental Health, 34(4), 143-149. https://doi.org/10.7870/cjcmh-2015-009

Atkinson, T. (2020, March). What it's like parenting a medically complex child during the coronavirus outbreak. Retrieved May 30, 2020, from https://themighty.com/2020/03/coronavirus-parenting-immunocompromised-child/?#conversation

Aylward, N. (2009). Access to education and training for young adult carers. National Institute of Adult Continuing Education. Retrieved June 1, 2020, from http://hdl.voced.edu.au/10707/47169

Barker, E., Greenberg, J., Seltzer, M., & Almeida, D. (2012). Daily stress and cortisol patterns in parents of adult children with a serious mental illness. Health Psychology, 31(1), 130–134. https://doi.org/10.1037/a0025325

Bibace and Walsh. (1980). Pediatrics. Vol. 66. P. 912

Brehaut, J.C., Kohen, D.E., Garner, R.E., Miller, A.R., Lach, L.M., & Klassen, A.F. (2009). Health among caregivers of children with health problems: findings from a Canadian population-based study. American Journal of Public Health, 99, 1254-1262.

Bridge the gApp. (n.d.). About Bridge to gApp. Retrieved June 17, 2020, from https://www.bridgethegapp.ca/youth/about-bridge-the-gapp/

Brooks, S.K., Webster, R.K., Smith, L.E., Woodland, L., Wessely, S., Greenberg, N. & Rubin, G.J. (2020). The psychological impact of quarantine and how to reduce it: rapid review of the evidence. Rapid Review, 395(10227), 912-920. https://doi.org/10.1016/S0140-6736(20)30460-8

Brody, J.A., Grant, M.D., Frateschi, L.J., Miller, S.C., Zhang, H., Reproductive Longevity and Increased Life Expectancy, Age and Ageing, 29, 75-78. https://pdfs.semanticscholar.org/6af4/2c1e6892fc0f8af5e3b8e3a8d609d790f302.pdf

Canadian Institute for Health Information. (2018). Almost half of unpaid caregivers of seniors with dementia experience distress. Retrieved May 28, 2020, from https://www.cihi.ca/en/almost-half-of-unpaid-caregivers-of-seniors-with-dementia-experience-distress

Cava, M.A., Fay, K.E., Beanlands, H.J., McCay, E.A., & Wignall, R. (2005). The experience of quarantine for individuals affected by SARS in Toronto. Public Health Nursing, 22(5), 398–406. https://doi.org/10.1111/j.0737-1209.2005.220504.x

Centers for Disease Control and Prevention. (n.d.-a). People who are at higher risk for severe illness. Retrieved May 28, 2020, from https://www.cdc.gov/coronavirus/2019-ncov/need-extra-precautions/people-at-higher-risk.html

Centers for Disease Control and Prevention. (n.d.-b). People with disabilities. Retrieved May 28, 2020, from https://www.cdc.gov/coronavirus/2019-ncov/need-extra-precautions/people-with-disabilities.html

Chatterji, S., Byles, J., Cutler, D., Seeman, T., & Verdes, E. (2015). Health, functioning, and disability in older adults - present status and future implications. Lancet, 385(9967), 563–575. https://doi.org/10.1016/S0140-6736(14)61462-8

Centers for Disease Control and Prevention. (n.d.-b). COVID-19 Guidance for Older Adults. Retrieved May 30, 2020 from www.cdc.gov/aging/covid19-guidance.html.

CNN. (2020). How to Decide Whether to Bring Your Elderly Parent Home from Assisted Living during the Pandemic. Retrieved June 15, 2020 from www.cnn.com/2020/03/30/health/parents-assisted-living-nursing-homes-coronavirus-wellness/index.html.

Crary, David. "Aging in Place: Most Seniors Want to Stay Put." MSNBC, Associated Press, 2011, philrichards.net/StayAtHomeInWilton/Aging%20in%20place%20-%20msnbc.pdf.

Crompton, S. (2015). What's stressing the stressed? Main sources of stress among workers. Statistics Canada. Retrieved June 25, 2020, from https://www150.statcan.gc.ca/n1/pub/11-008-x/2011002/article/11562-eng.htm#a5

Day, C. (2015). Young adult carers: a literature review informing the re-conceptualisation of young adult caregiving in Australia. Journal of Youth Studies, 18(7), 855-866. http://dx.doi.org/10.1080/13676 261.2014.1001826

Drucker, S.A. (2018, April 27). Betty Friedan: The three waves of feminism. Ohio Humanities. Retrieved June 25, 2020, from http://www.ohiohumanities.org/betty-friedan-the-three-waves-of-feminism/

Erikson, K. (1998). Trauma at Buffalo Creek. Societies, 35(2), 153-161.

Evans, Gary W. Environmental Stress. Cambridge U.P., 1984, 2-3.

Fairfax, A., Brehaut, J., Colman, I., Sikora, L., Kazakova, A., Chakraborty, P., & Potter, B. (2019). A systematic review of the association between coping strategies and quality of life among caregivers of children with chronic illness and/or disability. BMC Pediatrics. 19(215). https://doi.org/10.1186/s12887-019-1587-3

Feigin, R., Barnetz, Z., & Davidson-Arad, B. (2008). Quality of life in family members coping with chronic illness in a relative: An exploratory study. Families, Systems, & Health, 26(3), 267–281. https://doi.org/10.1037/a0013055

Foreign Policy. (2020, April). How the economy will look after the Coronavirus pandemic. Retrieved June 9, 2020, from https://foreignpolicy.com/2020/04/15/how-the-economy-will-look-after-the-coronavirus-pandemic/

George, A., Vickers, M.H., Wilkes, L., & Barton, B. (2008). Working and caring for a child with chronic illness: Challenges in maintaining employment. Employee Responsibilities and Rights Journal, 20, 165–176. https://doi.org/10.1007/s10672-008-9065-3

Giddens, A. (1990). The consequences of modernity. Polity, Cambridge.

Giroux, H. (2006). Reading Hurricane Katrina: Race, class, and the biopolitics of disposability. College Literature, 33(3), 171-196. Retrieved May 30, 2020, from www.jstor.org/stable/25115372

Good Therapy. (2019, March 15). Self-actualization. Retrieved June 25, 2020, from https://www.goodtherapy.org/learn-about-therapy/issues/self-actualization

Gould Soloway, R.A. (n.d.). Mold 101: Effects on human health. Poison Control: National Capital Poison Center. Retrieved June 17, 2020, from https://www.poison.org/articles/2011-oct/mold-101-effects-on-human-health

Government of Canada. (2014). Profile of Seniors in Canada. Retrieved June 5, 2020, from https://www.canada.ca/en/

employment-social-development/programs/seniors-action-report.html

Government of Canada. (2020-a). COVID-19 and people with disabilities in Canada. Retrieved June 3, 2020, from https://www.canada.ca/en/public-health/services/diseases/2019-novel-coronavirus-infection/guidance-documents/people-with-disabilities.html

Government of Canada. (2020-b). Resources for Canadians living with pain during COVID-19. Retrieved June 3, 2020, from https://www.canada.ca/en/health-canada/corporate/about-health-canada/public-engagement/external-advisory-bodies/resources.html#wb-auto-5

Government of Canada. (2020-c). Coronavirus disease (COVID-19): Symptoms and treatment. Retrieved June 9, 2020, from https://www.canada.ca/en/public-health/services/diseases/2019-novel-coronavirus-infection/symptoms.html?topic=ex-col-faq#a

Government of Canada. (2020). Mental Health and COVID-19 for public servants: Caregiving while working. Retrieved June 1, 2020, from https://www.canada.ca/en/government/publicservice/covid-19/caregiving-working.html

Gunn, K. (2020, April 8). Indigenous peoples and COVID-19: Protecting people, protecting rights. First Peoples Law. Retrieved June 17, 2020, from https://www.firstpeopleslaw.com/index/articles/449.php

Hawkins, R. L., & Maurer, K. (2011). 'You fix my community, you have fixed my life': the disruption and rebuilding of ontological security in New Orleans. Disasters, 35(1), 143–159. https://doi.org/10.1111/j.1467-7717.2010.01197.x

Hawryluck, L., Gold, W. L., Robinson, S., Pogorski, S., Galea, S., & Styra, R. (2004). SARS control and psychological effects of quarantine, Toronto, Canada. Emerging Infectious Diseases, 10(7), 1206–1212. https://doi.org/10.3201/eid1007.030703

Heston, J, et al. "Our Family, Our Way: Impact Of A Structured Guide On Family Caregiving Communication Barriers." Innovation in Aging, vol. 2, no. suppl_1, 2018, pp. 21–22., doi:10.1093/geroni/igy023.078.

Hochschild, A., & Machung, A. (1989). The second shift: Working families and the revolution at home. Penguin.

Hussain, R., Wark, S., & Ryan, P. (2018). Caregiving, employment and social isolation: Challenges for rural carers in Australia. International Journal of Environmental Research and Public

Health, 15(10), 2267. https://doi.org/10.3390/ijerph15102267
Indigenous Corporate Training Inc. (2018, February 12). 8 things you need to know about on-reserve housing issues. Retrieved June 17, 2020, from https://www.ictinc.ca/blog/8-things-you-need-to-know-about-on-reserve-housing-issues
International Disability Alliance. (2020). "We fall through the cracks". Stories from two women with psychosocial disabilities from the United States. Retrieved June 4, 2020, from http://www.internationaldisabilityalliance.org/covid19-usa
Jeong, H., Yim, H. W., Song, Y. J., Ki, M., Min, J. A., Cho, J., & Chae, J. H. (2016). Mental health status of people isolated due to Middle East Respiratory Syndrome. Epidemiology and Health, 38. https://doi.org/10.4178/epih.e2016048
Kantis, C., Kiernan, S., & Bardi, J.S. (2020). Updated: Timeline of the coronavirus. Think Global Health. Retrieved June 9, 2020, from https://www.thinkglobalhealth.org/article/updated-timeline-coronavirus
Kepreotes, E., Keatinge, D., & Stone, T. (2010). The experience of parenting children with chronic health conditions: A new reality. Journal of Nursing and Healthcare of Chronic Illness, 2(1), 51-62. https://doi.org/10.1111/j.1752-9824.2010.01047.x
Kim, J., Ingersoll-Dayton, B., & Minyoung, K. (2013). Balancing eldercare and employment: The role of work interruptions and supportive employers. Journal of Applied Gerontology, 32(3), 347-369. https://doi.org/10.1177/0733464811423647
Kimmel, M.S., & Holler, J. (2017). The gendered society (2nd ed.). Oxford University Press.
Lancet Public Health. (2020). Covid-19 and the consequences of isolating the elderly. Retrieved May 28, 2020 from https://www.thelancet.com/journals/lanpub/article/PIIS2468-2667(20)30061-X/fulltext
Lee, M. & Blanchard, T.C. (2011). Community attachment and negative affective states in the context of the BP Deepwater Horizon disaster. American Behavioral Scientist, 56(1), 24-47.
Lee, V. (2009). From Caregiving to Bereavement:Weaving the Strands of Identity. Retrieved June 8, 2020 from mro.massey.ac.nz/bitstream/handle/10179/1314/02whole.pdf?
Leonard, B., Brust, J. D., & Sapienza, J. J. (1992). Financial and time costs to parents of severely disabled children. Public Health Reports, 107(3), 302–312.
Lin, C., Tsai, Y., & Chang, H. (2008). Coping mechanisms of parents

of children recently diagnosed with autism in Taiwan: A qualitative study. Journal of Clinical Nursing, 17(20), 2733–2740. doi:10.1111/j.1365-2702.2008.02456.x

Lorenzi, C. (2020). Non voglio morire solo. La paura ai tempi del virus. QN Quotidiano Nazionale La Nazione, 80(9). [in Italian]

Lowenstein, E. (2018). A knock on the door. Journal of Loss & Trauma, 23(1), 44–50. https://0-doi-org.aupac.lib.athabascau.ca/10.1080/15325024.2017.1421413

LTC Responses to COVID-19. (2020). Impact of COVID-19 on Residents of Canada's Long-Term Care Homes - Ongoing Challenges and Policy Response. Retrieved June 12, 2020 from ltccovid.org/2020/04/15/impact-of-covid-19-on-residents-of-canadas-long-term-care-homes-ongoing-challenges-and-policy-response/.

Marazziti, D., & Stahl, S.M. (2020). The relevance of COVID-19 pandemic to psychiatry. World Psychiatry, 19(2), 261. https://doi.org/10.1002/wps.20764

Matthewman, S. (2016). Disasters, risks and revelation: Making sense of our time. Palgrave Macmillan.

Macdonald, M., & Lang, A. (2014). Applying risk society theory to findings of a scoping review on caregiver safety. Health and Social Care, 22(2), 124-133. https://doi.org/10.1111/hsc.12056

Mayall, Barry (Ed.). (1994).Children's Childhoods Observed and Experienced. "Responsible Children? Aspects of Children's Work and Employment Outside School in Contemporary UK. Morrow, Virginia." The Falmer Press.

McKeever, P. (1995). Between women: Nurses and family caregivers. Canadian Journal of Nursing Research, 26(4), 15-21.

McPhearson, D. A. (2020). Violating stay-at-home orders directly harms Disabled folks, but what else is new? Retrieved June 4, 2020, from https://blackyouthproject.com/violating-stay-at-home-orders-directly-harms-disabled-folks-but-what-else-is-new/

Measles & Rubella Initiative. (n.d.). The anti-vaccination movement. Retrieved June 25, 2020, from https://measlesrubellainitiative.org/anti-vaccination-movement/

Moyser, M. (2017). Women and paid work. Statistics Canada. Retrieved June 15, 2020, from https://www150.statcan.gc.ca/n1/pub/89-503-x/2015001/article/14694-eng.htm

Moyser, M. and Burlock, A. (2018). Women in Canada: A gender-based statistical guide. "Time use: Total work burden, unpaid work, and leisure."

Mucci, F., Mucci, N., Diolaiuti, F. (2020). Lockdown and isolation: Psychological aspects of COVID-19 pandemic in the general population. Clinical Neuropsychiatry, 17(2), 63-64. https://doi.org/10.36131/CN20200205

National Institute of Allergy and Infectious Diseases. (2020, May). Coronaviruses. Retrieved June 25, 2020, from https://www.niaid.nih.gov/diseases-conditions/coronaviruses

National Institute of Health. (2011, October). Community immunity: How vaccines protect us all. Retrieved June 25, 2020, from https://newsinhealth.nih.gov/2011/10/community-immunity

National Investment Center. (2019). Health Affairs Study: More Than Half of Middle-Income Seniors Will Lack Financial Resources for Seniors Housing and Care by 2029. Retrieved June 23, 2020 from https://www.norc.org/NewsEventsPublications/PressReleases/Pages/more-than-half-of-middle-income-seniors-will-lack-financial-resources-for-seniors-housing-and-care-by-2029

National Opinion Research Center. (2014). Long term care in America: Expectations and realities. http://www.longtermcarepoll.org/PDFs/LTC%202014/AP-NORC-Long-Term%20Care%20in%20America_FINAL%20WEB.pdf

Norris, F., & Elrod, C. (2006). Psychosocial consequences of disaster: A review of past research. In F. Norris, S. Galea, M. Friedman, et al. (Eds.), Methods for disaster mental health research (pp. 20-42). New York: Guilford.

Ontario Caregiver Organization. (2020). Caregiver Mental Health During COVID-19 Outbreak. Retrieved June 22, 2020 from https://ontariocaregiver.ca/wp-content/uploads/2020/03/Ontario-Caregiver-Organization-Caregiver-Mental-Health-During-COVID-19.pdf

Ontario Human Rights Commission. (n.d.). Ageism and age discrimination. Retrieved June 25, 2020 from http://www.ohrc.on.ca/en/ageism-and-age-discrimination-fact-sheet

Ontario Human Rights Commission. (n.d.). Policy on ableism and discrimination based on disability: What is disability? Retrieved May 27, 2020, from http://www.ohrc.on.ca/en/policy-ableism-and-discrimination-based-disability/2-what-disability

Open Text BC. (n.d.). Maslow's hierarchy of needs. Retrieved June 25, 2020, from https://opentextbc.ca/businessopenstax/chapter/maslows-hierarchy-of-needs/

Owermohle, S. (2020). Politico. "The 'biggest challenge' won't come until after a coronavirus vaccine is found." May 2020.

Palmer, D.E. (2020, March). Coronavirus comments expose underbelly of ageism, ableism. Retrieved May 30, 2020, from https://www.abilities.ca/opinion/coronavirus-comments-expose-underbelly-of-ageism-ableism/

Patterson, D. & Dyck, L. (2015, February). Housing on First Nation reserves: Challenges and successes. Interim Report of the Standing Senate Committee on Aboriginal Peoples. Retrieved June 17, 2020, from https://sencanada.ca/content/sen/Committee/412/appa/rep/rep08feb15b-e.pdf

Pellecchia, U., Crestani, R., Decroo, T., Van den Bergh, R., & Al-Kourdi, Y. (2015). Social consequences of Ebola containment measures in Liberia. PloS One, 10(12). https://doi.org/10.1371/journal.pone.0143036

Personal Genetics Education Project. (n.d.). What is eugenics? Retrieved June 2, 2020, from https://pged.org/history-eugenics-and-genetics/

Petretto, Donatella Rita, and Roberto Pili. "Ageing and COVID-19: What Is the Role for Elderly People?" Geriatrics, vol. 5, no. 2, 2020, p. 25., doi:10.3390/geriatrics5020025.

Pickup, Laurie. Built Environment, Women and the Environment (1984). "Women's Gender Role and its Influence on Travel Behaviour." 1984, Vol 10, No. 1., pp. 61-68. Published by Alexandrine Press.

Posen, A. (2020, April). How the economy will look after the Coronavirus pandemic. Foreign Policy. Retrieved June 9, 2020, from https://foreignpolicy.com/2020/04/15/how-the-economy-will-look-after-the-coronavirus-pandemic/

Public Health Agency of Canada. (2013, October). Chronic diseases. https://cbpp-pcpe.phac-aspc.gc.ca/chronic-diseases/

Reppermund, S., & Trollor, J. N. (2016). Successful ageing for people with an intellectual disability. Current Opinion in Psychiatry, 29(2), 149–154. https://doi.org/10.1097/YCO.0000000000000228

Rothan, Hussin A., and Siddappa N. Byrareddy. "The Epidemiology and Pathogenesis of Coronavirus Disease (COVID-19) Outbreak." Journal of Autoimmunity, vol. 109, 2020, p. 102433., doi:10.1016/j.jaut.2020.102433.

Sabucedo, J., Arce, C., Ferraces, M., Merino, H., & Duran, M. (2009). Psychological impact of the Prestige catastrophe. International Journal of Clinical and Health Psychology, 9, 105-116.

Sanderson, C., Lobb, E., Mowll, J., Butow, P., McGowan, N., & Price, M. (2013). Signs of posttraumatic stress disorder in caregivers following an unexpected death: A qualitative study. Palliative Medicine, 27(7), 625–631. https://doi.org/10.1177/0269216313483663

Schuck, P. (2020, May 5). Why community matters more than ever for parents of kids with special needs. CBC. https://www.cbc.ca/parents/learning/view/why-community-matters-more-than-ever-for-parents-of-kids-with-special-needs

Schwab and Lew-Williams. (2016).Wiley Interdisciplinary Review of Cognitive Science. "Language learning, socioeconomic status, and child-directed speech.", 2016. 2016 Jul; 7(4): 264–275

Sinha, M. (2013). Portrait of caregivers, 2012. Statistics Canada. https://www150.statcan.gc.ca/n1/en/pub/89-652-x/89-652-x2013001-eng.pdf?st=RmLVakjo

Skye, C. (2020, May 12). Colonialism of the curve: Indigenous communities & bad Covid data. Yellowhead Institute. Retrieved June 17, 2020, from https://yellowheadinstitute.org/2020/05/12/colonialism-of-the-curve-indigenous-communities-and-bad-covid-data/

Smith, L. (n.d.). #Ableism. Center for Disability Rights. Retrieved June 25, 2020, from http://cdrnys.org/blog/uncategorized/ableism/

Son, Juheui, et al. "The Caregiver Stress Process and Health Outcomes." Journal of Aging and Health, vol. 19, no. 6, 2007, pp. 871–887., doi:10.1177/08898264307308568.

Statistics Canada. (2009). Seniors. https://www150statcan.gc.ca/n1/pub/11-402-x/2011000/chap/seniors-aines/seniors-aines-eng.htm

Statistics Canada. (2012). Informal Caregiving for Seniors. https://www150.statcan.gc.ca/n1/en/catalogue/82-003-X201200311694

Statistics Canada. (2014-a). Time spent providing care to a family member or friend with a long-term illness, disability or aging needs by sex and age group. https://doi.org/10.25318/4410000601-eng

Statistics Canada. (2014-b). Time spent providing care to a family member or friend with a long-term illness, disability or aging needs by sex and main activity of respondent. https://doi.org/10.25318/4410000801-eng

Statistics Canada. (2015). Changing profile of stay-at-home parents. https://www150.statcan.gc.ca/n1/pub/11-630-x/11-630-x2016007-eng.htm

Statistics Canada. (2016-a). Population providing care to a family member or friend with a long-term illness, disability or aging needs by sex and main activity of respondent. https://doi.org/10.25318/4410000301-eng

Statistics Canada. (2016-b). Population providing care to a family member or friend with a long-term illness, disability or aging needs by sex and relationship between respondent and primary care receiver. https://doi.org/10.25318/4410000501-eng

Statistics Canada. (2017). Aboriginal peoples in Canada: Key results from the 2016 census. https://www150.statcan.gc.ca/n1/daily-quotidien/171025/dq171025a-eng.htm?indid=14430-1&indgeo=0

Statistics Canada. (2018). Canadian survey on disability (CSD). https://www23.statcan.gc.ca/imdb/p2SV.pl?Function=getSurvey&SDDS=3251

Statistics Canada. (2018). Caregivers in Canada. https://www150.statcan.gc.ca/n1/daily-quotidien/200108/dq200108a-eng.htm

Statistics Canada. (2019). Canadian survey on disability, 2017: Data visualization tool. https://www150.statcan.gc.ca/n1/pub/71-607-x/71-607-x2019035-eng.htm

Statistics Canada. (2020-a). Severity of disability for persons with disabilities aged 15 years and over, by age group and sex, Canada, provinces and territories. https://www150.statcan.gc.ca/t1/tbl1/en/tv.action?pid=1310037501

Statistics Canada. (2020-b). Type of disability for persons with disabilities aged 15 years and over, by age group and sex, Canada, provinces and territories. https://doi.org/10.25318/1310037601-eng

Statistics Canada. (2020-c). Total income for adults with and without disabilities. https://doi.org/10.25318/1310035601-eng

Statistics Canada. (2020-d). Total income for adults with disabilities. https://doi.org/10.25318/1310073101-eng

Statistics Canada. (2020-e). Old age security pension and guaranteed income supplement income for adults with disabilities. https://doi.org/10.25318/1310073201-eng

Statistics Canada. (2020-f). Labour force characteristics by sex and detailed age group, monthly, unadjusted for seasonality. https://doi.org/10.25318/1410001701-eng

Stiglitz, J.E. (2020, April). How the economy will look after the Coronavirus pandemic. Foreign Policy. Retrieved June 9, 2020, from https://foreignpolicy.com/2020/04/15/how-the-economy-will-look-after-the-coronavirus-pandemic/

Taanila, A., Syrajala, L., Kokkonen, J., & Jarvelin, M. R. (2002). Coping of parents with physically and/or intellectually disabled children. Child: Care, Health and Development, 28(1), 73–86.

Thorne, S., McCormick, J., & Carty, E. (1997). Deconstructing the gender neutrality of chronic illness and disability. Health Care for Women International, 18(1), 1–16.

Tierney, K.J. (2007). From the margins to the mainstream? Disaster research at the crossroads. Annual Review of Sociology, 33, 503-525. https://doi.org/10.1146/annurev.soc.33.040406.131743

Tufts Health Plan. (n.d.). The importance of good nutrition. Retrieved June 25, 2020, from https://www.tuftsmedicarepreferred.org/healthy-living/expert-knowledge/importance-good-nutrition

Tyson, L.D. (2020, April). How the economy will look after the Coronavirus pandemic. Foreign Policy. Retrieved June 9, 2020, from https://foreignpolicy.com/2020/04/15/how-the-economy-will-look-after-the-coronavirus-pandemic/

United Nations Development Program. (n.d.). COVID-19 pandemic: Humanity needs leadership and solidarity to defeat the coronavirus. Retrieved June 9, 2020, from https://www.undp.org/content/undp/en/home/coronavirus.html

Ursano, R., Fullerton, C., & Terhakopian, A. (2008). Disasters and health: Distress, disorders, and disaster behaviors in communities, neighborhoods, and nations. Social Research, 75, 1015-1028

Vacek, Pavel, Rybenská. "The Most Frequent Difficulties Encountered by Senior Citizens While Using Information and Communication Technology." Procedia – Social and Behavioral Sciences, vol. 217, 2016, pp. 452-458., doi:10.1016/j.sbspro.2016.02.013

Van der Velden, P., Grievink, L., Kleber, R., Drogendijk, A., Roskam, A.J., Marcelissen, F., Gersons, B. (2006). Post-disaster mental health problems and the utilization of mental health services: A four-year longitudinal comparative study. Administration and Policy in Mental Health and Mental Health Services Research, 33, 279-288.

Vitaliano, P.P., Young, H.M., & Zhang, J. (2004). Is caregiving a risk factor for illness? American Psychology Society, 13(1), 13-16. https://doi.org/10.1111/j.0963-7214.2004.01301004.x

World Health Organization. (2018). Managing epidemics: key facts about major deadly diseases. Geneva.

World Health Organization. (n.d.). Disabilities. Retrieved May 27, 2020, from https://www.who.int/topics/disabilities/en/

World Health Organization. (n.d.-b). What do we mean by self-care? Retrieved June 25, 2020, from https://www.who.int/reproductivehealth/self-care-interventions/definitions/en/

World Health Organization. (2020, April 15). Q&A: Violence against women during COVID-19. Retrieved June 25, 2020, from https://www.who.int/emergencies/diseases/novel-coronavirus-2019/question-and-answers-hub/q-a-detail/violence-against-women-during-covid-19?gclid=Cj0KCQjwudb3BRC9ARIsAEa-vUsc6sMZtLxcqvabw_rDTMOUGi1a4xgXuhM4jqO2ZidCsN3mf0Oh6Y4aAmTSEALw_wcB

World Health Organization. (2020). #HealthyAtHome – Mental Health. Retrieved June 15 from https://www.who.int/campaigns/connecting-the-world-to-combat-coronavirus/healthyathome/healthyathome---mental-health?

Ysseldyk, R., Kuran, N., Powell, S., & Villeneuve, P.J. (2019). Self-reported health impacts of caregiving by age and income among participants of the Canadian 2012 General Social Survey. Health Promotion and Chronic Disease Prevention in Canada, 39(5). https://doi.org/10.24095/hpcdp.39.5.01

YW Boston. (2017, March 29). What is intersectionality, and what does it have to do with me? Retrieved June 15, 2020, from https://www.ywboston.org/2017/03/what-is-intersectionality-and-what-does-it-have-to-do-with-me/

Xiang, Yu-Tao, et al. "Timely Mental Health Care for the 2019 Novel Coronavirus Outbreak Is Urgently Needed." The Lancet Psychiatry, vol. 7, no. 3, 2020, pp. 228–229., doi:10.1016/s2215-0366(20)30046-8.

www.ingramcontent.com/pod-product-compliance
Lightning Source LLC
Chambersburg PA
CBHW020432220526
45464CB00002B/676